RIGHT FOR YOU

Structure Your Thinking, Make a Decision, and
Move Forward with Your Career (and Life)

Lindsay Gordon

IS THIS BOOK RIGHT FOR YOU?

"As an engineering leader for several decades, I've seen up close what can happen when key staff get stuck in a rut and become distracted by where to go next in their careers. Lindsay's analytical and thoughtful approach is excellent at helping individuals in such a state. Her tools shine a spotlight on what matters to them and then how one can forge a plan to get there. A bonus to the company is her methods reduce the risk of losing key employees."

- Andy Scott, Engineering Director (ex-Google/Yahoo!/startups)

"Lindsay's ability to deliver focused, engaging, inspiring, and on-point career guidance to an audience with myriad needs and goals is a rare gift. When I consider speakers or coaches to work with my new hires, or myself, Lindsay is at the very top of my list. Lindsay provides refreshing guidance for us all as we seek to redefine how work fits into our lives."

- Kate Dey, Director at DocuSign

"I've dealt with Lindsay professionally for over a decade. When she put out her shingle as a career coach, I knew she'd succeed. But what has astonished me, is the impact she has on people's whole lives. Not just their career. Often, our work is our purpose. And our purpose is what gets us out of bed each day, ready to charge out and discover the world and our place in it. That's what Lindsay – and this book does – it can change your whole life."

- Glenn Riseley, Founder & CEO at HeadUp Labs

"Engineering is an enabler that allows people to solve complex real-world problems. It's a way of thinking about the world that goes beyond finding solutions and provides a mindset for tackling everyday life. In this book, Lindsay applies that engineering mindset to careers and offers a broader framework for how to think about your work."

- Gilda A. Barabino PhD, President of Olin College of Engineering

Do you hold out hope repeatedly banging your head against the corporate ladder will bring recognition beyond your paycheck? If you care so much about work that job dissatisfaction and disappointments jumble any rational career thoughts into extremes, Lindsay is an expert at efficiently unpacking this mess, helping you make some sense of it and identifying a way forward in career-land that is right for you."

- Heather M. Scott, Executive News Producer

"Lindsay Gordon makes people's lives better. Her "Right for YOU" tells you how. Read this and make its messages part of your thinking. I recommend it to my clients, students, and to you!"

- Gregg Jones, Crisis Management Consultant and Educator

Is This Book Right For You

"Lindsay's book is an eye opener. She demonstrates how your interests influence the work you enjoy through a strengths assessment and explores how your interests relate to job families and opportunities. I feel like reading it all over again."

- Suhita Singh, Technical Program Manager

"After a series of jobs at the same company for over 20 years, I needed to figure out my next career move. Lindsay helped me develop a clear picture of what I bring to the table, how my values are honored in a work environment, and the tools to confidently pursue a job that is right for me. If you are wondering if your current job still works for you, the combination of Lindsay's structured exercises and unwavering support can help you quiet the questions in your head and create a path for the future."

- Jennifer Fischer, Senior Product Management Leader

"Lindsay Gordon is a magician. As a former engineer, she knows exactly the right systems to put in place for each of her clients and the precise questions to ask you that get you to dig deep and figure out what works for YOU as a way of life! Lindsay taught me to evaluate the companies I interviewed with just as much as they were evaluating me. This turned out to be a great lesson for life overall. I always recommend her to friends and colleagues at all levels - she is transformative and will get you confident and clear!"

- Katiana Krawchenko, Broadcast Director at Subject Matter

"As someone who appreciates a structured process with tailored guidance, resources, frameworks, and plenty of direct interaction with thought-provoking conversations, Lindsay's coaching program and style were a great fit for me. She helped me trust the process, and I enjoyed putting in the time and energy to achieve my own "unsexy" results which continue to serve me through career and life decisions!"

- Andrea Siefers, Senior Engineer at Geosyntec Consultants

"When I first spoke with Lindsay, I felt stuck. I was uninspired, lacked conviction in my own abilities, and was wondering if I had peaked in my career. Over the course of working with her, I was able to uncover my intrinsic motivations, deeply understand my priorities, and figure out what makes me tick. With that clarity in hand, I've made the changes I needed to not only get out of the rut but truly be able to lead a life that's unabashedly me."

- Vishal Iyer, Design Manager at Meta

"Lindsay taught me a skillset around HOW to make decisions clearly and confidently that I not only used for the next step in my career, but continue to use in all aspects of my life. Lindsay's work is unique in that it teaches you a framework to evaluate why you're not happy in your career, and how to make decisions about the next step. Anyone who wants to learn how to make clear and confident decisions about all aspects of their lives (career, moving to a new country, buying a house, etc) would benefit from learning Lindsay's framework."

- Zahra Ghofraniha, Software Engineer at Google

First published in 2022 by Lindsay Gordon

© Lindsay Gordon

Author: Gordon, Lindsay
Title: Right for YOU: Structure Your Thinking, Make a Decision, and Move Forward with Your Career (and Life)
ISBN: 978-1-4710-9628-0

Editor-in-chief: Rachel Koontz
Cover Design: Sarah Rose Graphic Design
Photographer: Stanley Desbas Photography

Disclaimer:
The material in this publication is of the nature of general professional advice, but it is not intended to provide specific guidance for particular circumstances and it should not be relied on as the basis for any decision to take action or not take action on any particular matter which it covers. Readers should obtain individual advice from the author where appropriate, before making any such decision. To the maximum extent permitted by law, the author and publisher disclaim all responsibility and liability to any person, arising directly or indirectly from any person taking or not taking action based on the information in this publication.

To my clients.

Thank you for showing us the way by courageously doing what was right for you.

TABLE OF CONTENTS

FOREWORD

Many people define themselves by the work they do, so the prospect of potentially changing jobs (or careers) is scary because it calls into question big chunks of our own visions of who we are. If you are reading this book then there's a pretty good chance you are facing exactly this existential crisis.

You also probably already have an idea that the most commonly offered career planning advice is wrong. Not just wrong, in fact, but deeply counterproductive and harmful. The entire space (in my opinion) is heavy on meaningless platitudes and light on useful ideas. As someone who has been hiring and growing people for nearly 30 years it makes me angry to see people facing legitimately difficult choices unnecessarily twisted into knots by the hand waving banalities of hucksters.

Enter Lindsay Gordon.

I have been lucky to know Lindsay since 2014 and have witnessed firsthand her determined transformation from "nervous seeker" to "confident guide." We worked together at Google when she went through her own existential crisis of meaning and I have watched with great interest (and no small measure of admiration) as she found her own way and dedicated herself to helping others do the same.

I'm sure she will have her own view of her origin story, but for me it all started one afternoon when Lindsay came into my office, sat down across from me, looked me intently in the eyes and said "I'm unhappy and I don't know why but I'm going to go figure it out."

For the record, this is not something a manager wants to ever hear from someone working for them - especially someone doing a really good job!

But... There we were.

The most memorable thing to me was her resoluteness. She wasn't asking for help. She was telling me simply and plainly that she'd had enough of feeling unfulfilled and she was going to go fix it – no matter where that led.

Fast forward several years and today she has helped hundreds of people find meaning in their work and – by extension – more meaning in their lives.

This book isn't very long because Lindsay gets right to the point. There is no one-size-fits-all way to have a career that gives you meaning, but there are a set of frameworks you can use to figure out what's right for you. That's what Lindsay will teach you.

Foreword

These decisions may seem scary and the choices may seem endlessly complicated, but they don't have to be. The only decision you really have to make is whether or not you're willing to commit yourself to your own happiness. In truth, the only wrong choice you can make is continuing to do something that leaves you unfulfilled.

Maybe you should find more meaning in the work you are already doing, or maybe it's time for you to find something new to do. I don't know, but Lindsay will help you figure that out if you let her.

Whatever you finally decide, just know that the time and effort you spend in the next 150 pages will pay for itself nearly instantly and the value you get will compound for the rest of your career. As investments go, you can't do much better than that.

Good luck in your search and I hope you find the meaning you seek.

David K. Rensin
Los Altos, CA
August 2022

A NOTE FROM THE AUTHOR

Hundreds of people have come to me in their lowest moments when they felt like they had nowhere left to turn. They've shared their deepest regrets, their greatest fears, and their biggest dreams. On the surface, I often hear stories about career dissatisfaction, but many people soon realize that it's so much deeper than that. Their dissatisfaction with their work is impacting their families, their mental health, the kind of parent they want to be, their sense of self, their ability to find a partner, their relationship with alcohol, their marriages, and the potential that they always saw for themselves. I'm humbled by the experience of bearing witness to things they've never told another soul about the life they hoped they would be living. It's a humbling experience seeing people come to terms with how long they've felt this way and how quickly time has passed. It's a humbling experience to see people face the fact that they don't want to live the rest of their life this way.

It's changed me to see people not give up. To see people take such courageous action in their lives and to trust me with their tiny embers of hope that there has to be a better way. I've learned so much about how hard it can be to be a human in this world, and I've witnessed the most unbelievable courage too. I've seen again and again what it looks like for somebody to make decisions with confidence, to finally feel good in their own skin, and truly do what's right for them, and I feel compelled to share this wisdom with as many people as I can.

I want to honor the courage of everyone I've had the privilege to work with, and create a ripple effect bigger than they could have ever imagined when they first spoke with me. I want their courage to impact families, communities, and workplaces across the globe as more and more people start doing what's right for them. For every one person that shows up on my doorstep, there are 100 more that are hurting that I don't get the chance to meet.

I hope this book enables everyone to make decisions with clarity and confidence, do what's right for them, and feel fully alive in their work and life.

INTRODUCTION

I'm a highly successful career coach and I want to admit something to you: I have *no idea* what you should do with your career. None. Not at all. Not even one bit. Literally no clue.

And if I had to guess, you've already heard more than a few suggestions from others about what you should do, how you should feel about work, and what it should mean to you.

In my world, there's only one thing that matters. What YOU want.

If you want to stay at your company even though other people are warning you that you've become a "lifer?" **Awesome.**

If you want to make a big change away from the work you've been doing for decades and make a complete 180 from the "logical next step?" **Awesome.**

If you want to stay in a boring job that allows you to spend time, energy, and attention on things outside of work? **Awesome.**

You get to do what's right for YOU.

And instead of giving you answers, I believe you'll find what's right for you with a new framework for changing your thinking and restructuring your decision making.

THIS ISN'T YOUR TYPICAL BOOK ON CAREER DEVELOPMENT

I'm a customer-service-loving, engineering-degree-holding, fell-into-running-a-business career coach and I take professional baking classes because I kind of want to be a baker. I assure you, that does not create the conditions for standard career conversations.

I'm going to say things that may be wildly different from the way you've traditionally been taught to think about your career and things that you may not initially agree with, but I invite you to try them on and see what works for you.

Introduction

I'm tired of seeing people who have followed the external definitions of success by climbing the ladder, chasing money, job-hopping, and feeling incredibly empty about where that's gotten them.

I hate the advice to "quit your job and do your passion."

I don't think your meaning, purpose, and drive in life have to come from your work.

I wish other people would stop telling you what they think you should be doing without having any idea if it's right for you.

I desire a workplace where employees can have conversations with their employers about fit, instead of feeling like their only option is to quit, leaving the company no chance to re-engage them.

I deeply want to teach people to do what's right for them and I believe that racism, sexism, ageism, ableism, and other systemic barriers in the workplace get in the way of that.

I want to burn down the systemic barriers in the workplace that keep so many people from being able to "just be yourself!" at work. I want to create safety for employees to be able to express when they're not in the right spot and open a conversation about how to get there, whether that's at the company or not. I want a tailored understanding of what success looks like for each of us. Only then can we have a workplace and a world where people are engaged, contributing and fully alive.

This book is for people who spend a lot of time questioning the path they're on and wondering how to make the decision that is right for them. You're in the right place if you want to stop doing what you think is "right" and start doing what's right for you.

If you're looking for tactical support with a job search, industry-specific knowledge about certain career paths, or how to find success in the ways that society defines, this is not the book for you. If you're looking for someone to tell you the right answer, this is not the book for you.

But if you're willing to go through a process to uncover the answers that you already have? Do I have a framework for you!

Now, on the topic of delightful frameworks, this one has the power to revitalize not only your career but your *life*. If that sounds sensational, I get it, but my clients have shown that this works. As one person shared, "I now have life skills that will serve me for the rest of my life. Not just for the rest of my professional career, but in everyday life as well."

Yes, we will build the framework to help you make decisions about your career. This is what shows you the way to rebuild trust in your decision-making… and from there, you can apply the concepts to any and all areas of your life.

Introduction

What you're getting in this book has transformed the lives of many of my clients, from ages 18 to 68, from accountants to journalists, and from new grads to CEOs. The framework will help you cut through the noise of what everyone else thinks. It'll pull you out of the spiral that shows up when you talk to a recruiter, and it will help you talk to your manager about where you want to contribute at the company. I promise you that this framework will give you new ways to think about your career, help you structure your thinking, and get you out of the rut that you're stuck in. I like to call it, the Framework of Freedom.

Clearly, I *love* a good framework but I want you to know right up front that the framework is only half of the book. (Fun fact: I was once called a "framework creating machine" which, to me, felt like a badge of honor.) Don't say"... I didn't warn you! Don't worry, there will be lots of exercises and prompts, and feel free to create as many spreadsheets as you'd like, but the framework isn't everything here. What's equally important is that I share stories, rewire your thinking in several dimensions, challenge your conventional view of career, and provide context.

My hope is that I can integrate all of those things and help you:

1. Understand *why* you feel the way you do about your career (and release any sense of failure)

2. Align yourself to what matters most to you

3. Use the framework to shape your future decision-making

RIGHT FOR ME

"But Google is the number one place in the world to work!"

I didn't have to hear that response too many times before I started hiding how much I was struggling to fit in at Google. It was clear that I just couldn't hack it at the best company in the world and it seemed like I was the only one.

I spent 6 years working at Google and while there are many things that I am grateful for about the experience (great friends, amazing opportunities, and the best manager I've had), I struggled almost that entire time to find where I fit in. I was never the most technical and I also *loved* customer service (I literally went to conferences for customer service for fun). I had an engineering degree but didn't work as an engineer. I didn't feel like my unique combination of gifts ever squarely fit into one role and I waffled for years about what I should do. I tried to transfer internally but was unsuccessful because I couldn't articulate how my skills and experience would apply to a new part of the organization.

At one point, I almost accepted an external offer but turned it down last minute because I was afraid I would just jump into another place where I couldn't hack it. If I couldn't articulate why things weren't working at Google, what hope did I have for success at another company?

What I would have given for even *one person* to have a conversation with me and invite me to consider that Google just might not have been a good fit for me.

Rock bottom for me came four years into the job. I was still unhappy, had no idea what to do about it, and both my manager and colleague (rightfully) called me out on my terrible attitude. I started looking for any questions or prompts that would help me reflect on what was important to me and what I needed out of a job. I started finding the common threads between all the pieces of my background that felt all over the place. I cobbled together my own framework of freedom and I emerged with confidence, direction, energy, and a plan. I had the words to articulate the misalignment of fit, rather than the personal failure.

I decided at that moment that I never wanted anyone else to feel the way that I had, especially if their job looked shiny and perfect on paper or they worked at a big fancy company.

And I've dedicated the last 6 years of my life to making that happen.

Since then, my frameworks and ways of thinking have helped thousands of people. I've worked with senior leaders at companies from Apple to Wells Fargo to Johnson &

Johnson. I've spoken at the Grace Hopper Celebration (the world's largest gathering of women in computing), run workshops for companies, universities, and career platforms, and been featured on podcasts like, "How to Be Awesome at Your Job" and "Side Hustle School." I've worked with architects, lawyers, engineers, clothing designers, university administrators, literary editors, health professionals, and more. I'll keep sharing what I learned so that anyone who is ready can start making decisions that work for them.

SO... ARE YOU IN?

This is not a book about having it all figured out. It's not a book about landing the job.

This is a book about getting back in touch with yourself and what you want.

It's a guide for making decisions you know you'll be happy with.

It's about having the best conversation you've had with your manager and leadership team around fit and contributing in meaningful ways in your life and work.

Introduction

(And if you happen to be a manager or leader at your company, this is a book about how to support your people in meaningful and effective ways and truly do what's right for them)

If you're thinking, "Sign me up for that!" then let's dive in.

PART 1

STRUCTURE YOUR THINKING

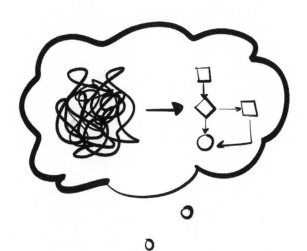

Right For YOU

You may gain an incredible amount of clarity and insight just by thinking about your career differently.

If you're like most of my clients, you're probably focused on what action you need to take to relieve your situation (Should I quit? Should I take the promotion? Should I change fields?) but I know that mindset shifts can be just as powerful as drastic change.

For example, we have to talk about the pressures you feel in a million different directions that make it so hard to listen to yourself. It's vital that we acknowledge the societal norms at play and how they are playing into your perspective and self-judgment. And I want to illuminate all the complicated parts that go into knowing what's right for you in your career while validating and honoring your wiring along with your fears.

I hope you're ready for a lot of reframing because that's truly half the process. A client said to me,

"I can't understate how much I appreciate your ability to reframe my thoughts and situations. It just took one of your quick reframes during our conversations for me to see myself or situation in a completely different light."

Let's get you some relief.

1. End the Waffling

If I could give everyone in this world a gift, it would be to relieve their indecision about their careers, to completely remove the pain that waffling creates for people.

I'm on a mission to help people restructure their thinking so they can make decisions and move forward to explore, experience, and live life. I unleash people to do what *they* want to do in this world and to have the experience of being fully alive.

I'm a career coach but I'm doing more than just helping you think about your job because I know that it's much bigger than that.

When you are undecided about your career, your life is on hold.

Not your career, your life. The indecision and resulting unhappiness at work inevitably leak into all the other parts of your life. You have little to no energy for yourself or your loved ones at the end of the day and you're not showing up as the person you want to be with your coworkers or your family members. You might be doing the bare minimum at work which affects both your output and your confidence in yourself. The stagnation breeds feelings of disengagement and inadequacy which further drain your energy and inspiration to make a change.

There's an incredible impact of being undecided that we don't talk about enough. If you've experienced this before, you know how exhausting it is to be stuck in a pattern of not knowing what you want and how to move forward.

For one of my clients, she considered quitting her job every single day. It was so exhausting to have the same conversation with herself day after day and it felt like it was taking over her life.

4

For another client, he had his resignation letter ready to go and felt at the edge of the cliff of quitting several times in his 20+ years at the company. Continually repeating the cycle of feeling tired of his role, wanting something else, thinking about starting a new job or business but ultimately ruling out the choice to quit had a detrimental effect on every relationship in his life.

For another, the cycle was incredibly predictable. He would scroll jobs on LinkedIn, get more confused about what he wanted and what he could do well, and then go back to his current work because he didn't have any other option. Coasting at work technically felt easy but it left him in a bad headspace.

The time and mental energy you spend waffling, regretting, second-guessing, beating yourself up about past decisions, and asking yourself the same questions over and over again is all-consuming.

I take the fact that we have crossed paths incredibly seriously. I know that your happiness is at stake because your current job disssatisfaction ultimately has an impact on many areas of your life. For you that may be your relationship with your partner, how you're showing up for your kids, your mental health, or the potential you want to live up to for yourself. I know what it feels like to have someone want to change their life and then call me two years later and let me know that they haven't taken a single action.

We don't know how much time we have. Your life is happening now, and I will do absolutely everything I can to get you DECIDED and return you to the feeling of being fully alive and engaged in your life.

THE NEVER-ENDING QUESTIONS

A client came to me years ago after a trip home to see her parents over the holidays. She was going through some of her belongings and found one of her old journals. She read a passage that she'd written 11 years prior, where she was talking about trying to figure out what she wanted to do with her life.

When she reached out to me, she shared,

"11 years later, while I've done a lot, I'm essentially still asking the same question. It kind of hit me right in the face that if I don't start being more intentional about my next moves, I could be asking the same question in another 10 years."

You may have been asking yourself the same question for a few months, a few years, or a few decades.

Do I need to leave the career that I identify with and that I've aspired to since childhood?

Have I stayed at this company for too long?

Could I be successful anywhere other than in my current field?

End the Waffling

Do I have to quit to be happy?

Am I even good at the career I've been doing for years?

I've always thought about going back to school for a completely different career. Is that truly what I want?

I once asked a client how long she'd been feeling the way she did about her career. Her answer amazed me.

"My entire career, to be honest," she said. *"I had these thoughts during my Ph.D. and then for the 14 years I have worked in industry. I just had no confidence or other path to pursue. So, I have just continued on this 'semi-successful' career. But the thought of pursuing this longer than 5 more years or so fills me with anxiety."*

Whatever your question and however long you've been asking it, I invite you to add lots of kindness and compassion for not being able to find the answer. You've come to the right place to get relief and a framework of how to structure your thinking and I promise you we will get you decided.

"I WISH I COULD CARE LESS."

If this thought has crossed your mind as a potential way to end your suffering, I get it... because I've been there.

When I was working at Google and struggling to figure out why I was so unhappy and didn't feel like I fit in, my best friend and I booked a conference room, laid down on the floor (yep, that definitely happened), and had some real talk. I was so frustrated about why I was unhappy. My complaining went something like this:

"Ughhhhhh! Google is the best place to work in the world, and everyone else seems to be happy. Why can't I just be happy not really enjoying my job? Why do I care so much? Can't I just care less?"

Thank goodness for good friends who call us out.

My friend looked at me and said,

"I'm sorry, is our goal to care less in this world? Is complacency what we're after?"

Her words have stuck with me for years and they live at the top of a career manifesto I wrote for myself that day.

"Complacency is not what we are after." - Lindsay Gordon

Let me be clear that this has nothing to do with the external pressure to do more, be more, produce at all costs, always be hustling, never be satisfied, etc. I'm talking about when *you*, internally, have a feeling that you want more for yourself out of your work.

When you're unhappy in your job, you may look around and see that everyone else seems fine with theirs. You might compare yourself to your partner and see them not be bothered by their boring job. Or you may have a friend who seems to be "putting up with" finding her meaning and drive outside of work. The quiet "sometimes I wish I could care less" can slip in so slowly.

Everything is fine, nothing is terribly wrong, why can't I be happy? Everyone else seems to be!

I compare myself to my spouse frequently because he is so easily satisfied. I do often think about why my standards have to be so high. Why can't I just be happy with having everything else in my life go well?

I see people who are happy and I think there must be something intrinsically wrong with me.

Here's what I learned on that day. Everyone gets to do what's right for them in their career. We don't need to make anyone around you wrong. *And,* the people around you might be up to something different than you are. We have no idea what other folks are dealing with, what they need out of their job, or what barriers they're facing in their work. "Everyone else is fine with it" isn't always true.

But if you're here, trying to care less as I was on that day at Google, I'm going to guess that caring less is not your answer. It adds the pressure that you should be feeling differently than you do. It's asking you to ignore how you feel and it takes so much energy to try to psyche yourself into a thing you don't want to be doing. It's double exhausting to be drained at work and to feel like you *should* feel better about it. It's out of alignment with who you are and what allows you to thrive and it crushes your soul and your desire to contribute.

I don't think we need people who care less in this world. I think we need more people who are aligned and alive in their careers and lives in ways that are meaningful to them. And we certainly need you and your contribution.

If you have a sense that deep down, caring less is not what you're craving either, you're in the right place.

WHAT'S YOUR ESCAPE HATCH?

As you think about the questions you've been asking yourself and your own cycle of waffling, I want you to see if there are any sneaky options you consider that I like to call the "escape hatch."

This is the daydream that comes back again and again. The "wouldn't it be great if I could just…"

Burn it all down and be a potter in the woods.

Move to an island and live off the grid.

Travel the world and have no possessions.

Insert your own version here.

Telling yourself a story is what allows you to be distracted and feeds your spiral. The constant "what if." Like this client:

"I did not have a sense of whether my current job was part of the career that I wanted. I spent a lot of time questioning the path I was on, giving attention to 'what-if' scenarios, and comparing myself to others."

Now, in my world, we don't actually need to dismiss these options as impractical or childish, we want to capture them and assess whether they work for you. Otherwise, they'll keep coming back day after day, year after year, fueling the continuing indecision.

Part of the work I do is help people cut down on the number of options they think they have. The truth is that yes, you could do anything, but in reality, you don't want to do everything. That's why we're going to build an incredibly tailored framework that allows you to make the decisions that are right for you. And you'll finally get to assess your escape hatch options, once and for all, to see if they're a distraction or a true desire.

ONE QUESTION? OR A MILLION?

When you have no idea what you want, there's no way you can communicate it to someone else.

This is evident when the interviewer is left with the feeling that you're not even sure if you want the job. It can also show up when your network is ready and willing to support you but you're not reaching out because you have no idea what to tell them and don't want to waste a conversation. It's painful to go to senior people without a direction or to not be able to answer your manager's dreaded question, "Well, what *do* you want?"

Why is it so incredibly hard to answer what seems like such a simple question?

You are not alone.

"With a recent career pivot within my company, I keep getting asked to define what I want. I'm afraid I'm losing the opportunity by not having a plan."

"My long career in business leaves me feeling stressed and without purpose, yet my attempt to answer the question 'What do I want to be when I grow up?' leaves me feeling lost."

"Without knowing what I want to do and being able to articulate it clearly, I can't move forward with looking for a new job. I am not controlling where my career is going and instead, letting the leaders and the company move me where they want, not where I want to go."

Part of the difficulty in knowing what you want is that you may be unable to articulate what's wrong with your current situation. It's sticky because there are a million questions tangled together:

Is the problem me?

Is it leadership?

Is it the culture?

Do I just hate the day-to-day work? My manager?

Is it the role? The company? The whole field?

If you could unlock the answers to these questions, you'd be able to confidently evaluate new opportunities or choose to stay exactly where you are. Ultimately, you want to answer this question, once and for all:

"What does job satisfaction look like for me, and can I cultivate it at my current company?"

One of my clients, a successful Program Manager at a tech company was questioning if she was at odds with her current company or at odds with her overall career path. She had no energy or motivation, and it was spilling over into her personal life. We discovered that she'd always been creative since childhood and one of her earliest dreams was to become a concept artist. Even though she hadn't done any art in over ten years, she started taking small steps to test out the idea of a career in concept art. Years later she shared her incredible artwork with me as she was getting ready to graduate from an art university. In her case, she was able to see that it wasn't just her current company; she had a desire to create a new path for herself.

Throughout this book, we'll be focusing on helping you articulate what's working and not working in your current situation. This allows you to either make changes that will make a real difference for you or confidently decide that this environment is not the right one for you.

The more that you can articulate what's not working, the more you can create an environment that will work.

THE FREEDOM OF BEING DECIDED

I truly believe that when you end your waffling, you get back to living your life.

There's an incredible peace that comes from knowing why you're making the choice you are and exactly why it works for you. No more arguing with yourself in your head and convincing yourself not to quit each day. You get to *choose* where you spend your mental energy and be 100 percent invested in whatever role you choose.

And remember when I said that the waffling leaks into the rest of your life and affects the lives of the people around you? Luckily, the opposite is true as well. When you're able to decide and feel confident about the choice you've made, it starts to leak into the rest of your life in a positive way.

As one client told me:

"I changed the things that weren't working for me in my current work situation and clarified for myself what I want to do in the next chapter of my career. My family, my co-workers, and I have greatly benefited because I'm a better and more authentic version of myself."

I'm really glad you're here so we can give you the freedom of being decided. I want you to start believing that the same results I've seen with my clients are just around the corner for you too. You'll learn throughout this process that it's not actually about having all the answers, but about having the tools to make decisions with clarity and confidence along the way.

And can I ask you for a favor? If this book sets you free to do what's right for you, share it and keep making the workplace and world around you a place where others can do the same.

2. Why It's Not Always as Simple as "Do What's Right for You!"

Alot of my work is helping people make decisions they know they'll be happy with and helping people do what's right for them in their careers. This can sound overly simplistic because there's often much more at play than just what they get to decide.

The question we also need to ask is, who doesn't get to be themselves at work? Who doesn't get to make decisions that honor their values and preferences? An attendee at one of my workshops framed it as, "What happens when the world makes it suck to be you—how do you work on designing around that?"

It would be naive to think that everyone could just "do what is right for them!" as the workplace (and world) is not set up for everyone to succeed. The dominant culture we live in has continually trained us to undervalue and override our own needs and desires in favor of what's best for those in power. Some of the systemic issues are more US-centric and others are global.

THE BIAS OF 'PROFESSIONALISM' STANDARDS

There is a bias built into standards of "professionalism" that often favors the values of white and Western employees, according to two American grassroots organizer-scholars, Dr. Tema Okun and Keith Jones[1]. This can affect how you're perceived by the way you dress, your language and vocabulary, your name, and much more.

Take natural Black hairstyles for example. UPS only lifted their discriminatory ban on natural Black hairstyles in 2020, before that it was against company policy to wear an

---

[1] https://ssir.org/articles/entry/the_bias_of_professionalism_standards

Afro or braids[2]. California was the first state to ban racial discrimination against natural hairstyles in the workplace in 2019, with the passing of the CROWN Act[3]. This legislation was created in partnership with then State Senator Holly J. Mitchell of California, who said,

"This is a fundamental issue of personal dignity and personal rights [...] This bill has truly struck a deeply personal chord with people because there is something so deeply personally offensive when you are told that your hair, in its natural state, is not acceptable in the workplace."

From the CROWN Act's website, Black women are 1.5 times more likely to be sent home from the workplace because of their hair. And Black women are 80% more likely than white women to agree with this statement: "I have to change my hair from its natural state to fit in at the office[4]."

They go on to say, "People should not be forced to divest themselves of their racial-cultural identity by changing their natural hair in order to adapt to predominantly white spaces in the workplace or in school."

But there are countless ways that employees are forced to adapt to predominantly white spaces and cultural norms.

---

[2] https://www.cnn.com/2020/11/11/business/ups-end-beard-ban/index.html

[3] https://www.nytimes.com/2019/06/28/us/natural-hair-discrimination-ban.html

[4] https://www.thecrownact.com/

Employees who speak with an accent have a lower chance of being hired or promoted to a higher position[5]. According to a research report from the Center for Talent Innovation, "more than 35% of Black and Hispanic employees, as well as 45% of Asian employees, say they "need to compromise their authenticity" to conform to their company's standards of demeanor or style."[6]

The US Equal Employment Opportunity Commission reported 36.1% of the employment discrimination claims in 2020 were disability-based[7]. Neurodiverse employees or employees with invisible disabilities are confused about when—or if—they should disclose it at work[8]. Transgender and nonbinary employees frequently experience harassment and discrimination in the workplace. The National Center for Transgender Equality reports that more than 1 in 4 transgender people have lost a job due to bias[9]. According to a 2020 study from the Center for American Progress, "more than one-third of LGBTQ Americans (35 percent) said their ability "to be hired" has been negatively affected

---

[5] https://www.forbes.com/sites/pragyaagarwaleurope/2018/12/30/bias-is-your-accent-holding-you-back/

[6] https://hbr.org/2012/10/too-many-people-of-color-feel

[7] https://www.eeoc.gov/statistics/data-visualization-disability-charges

[8] https://hbr.org/2021/06/make-it-safe-for-employees-to-disclose-their-disabilities; https://hbr.org/2019/06/why-people-hide-their-disabilities-at-work

[9] https://transequality.org/issues/employment

to a moderate or significant degree in the past year due to discrimination, along with about 3 in 10 people (31 percent) who have faced negative impacts on their "salary or ability to be promoted" or their "ability to retain employment."[10] The Future Forum's Remote Employee Experience Index found that for Black knowledge workers in the US, only 3% want to go back into the office full-time (versus 21% of their white colleagues)[11] and Ruchika Tulshyan, author of Inclusion on Purpose, says that "a return to in-person work will also mean a return to microaggressions, pressure to conform to white standards of professionalism, and high rates of workplace stress and burnout."[12]

While this is by no means an exhaustive list of the ways people are forced to adapt in the workplace, it gives you an idea of how many people are dealing with discrimination. Hiding parts of your identity, needing to transform your physical appearance, and dealing with harassment are all incredibly energy-draining emotional burdens even before we consider whether you enjoy your work.

As we go through this process, we will continue to acknowledge the systemic barriers that exist in the workplace

---

[10] https://www.americanprogress.org/article/state-lgbtq-community-2020/

[11] https://futureforum.com/2021/01/28/hybrid-rules-the-emerging-playbook-for-flexible-work/

[12] https://www.nytimes.com/2021/06/23/us/return-to-office-anxiety.html

and make sure that you're not attributing personal fault for something that is structural.

For example, when a client listened to a #SecureTheSeat podcast episode about creating boundaries in the workplace with Dr. Erin L. Thomas, the Vice President and Head of Diversity, Inclusion & Belonging at Upwork, it blew her away to connect the idea that immigrants have always had to earn their keep in this country and that is part of what can make setting boundaries so difficult[13].

For another client, she decided to leave her current environment. She joined a company that, as she said,

"truly values me, my experiences and doesn't have tiny hang-ups in culture that makes me feel less than."

Another client found peace in truly seeing the ways that her company was not a good fit after constantly feeling like her contributions were minimized. In a compassionate note to herself, she wrote,

"You've experienced all these micro-aggressions (and frankly, straight-up aggressions) that range from being told as a minority woman to be "more vulnerable" and "more resilient" while being held to a completely different standard. As much as they would've wanted to put the blame on you, you now understand that it wasn't just you — it was ultimately

---

[13] https://anchor.fm/minda-harts/episodes/Creating-Boundaries-in-the-workplace-w-special-guest-Dr--Erin-L--Thomas-e12scea

not a fit, in terms of values, working style, environment, role, or even type of work and topic."

I'll invite you to see what kind of support you need and to find your agency to do what's right for you while navigating the barriers you experience. And remember that your lived experience trumps any of the recommendations in this book. You are always the one that knows what's right for you.

WHEN A PROMOTION IS A TRAP

There's a lot of pressure to just go along with the norm or take the expected path of least resistance in our careers. One area where that shows up is continuing to climb the ladder. We see a promotion as a cause for celebration—more money, a better title, more responsibilities—but when is it not? For several of my clients, being offered a promotion actually felt like a trap.

Take this conversation for example:

"I'm very well respected at my job and everyone always raves about how much they enjoy working with me, but I don't feel that. I don't feel like I do anything important, and I can't even efficiently articulate what I do."

Doing work that doesn't feel important or meaningful to you is already a very energy-draining situation to be in. But it turns out that getting recognized for that work, actually makes it feel worse. There can be a huge disconnect when you're not happy with your work product but others are telling you you're doing a great job. You get recognized for work that you're not proud of or that may fall into the "you're good at it" category but not the "you enjoy doing it" category. Or you're showing up mostly checked out, firing at 25 percent capacity, and people are raving about you? How do you reconcile that?

Another client said it this way. He received a promotion earlier in the year with a nice salary bump but he feels even worse now. He's doing the same thing as before but now feels like he has more pressure since he's being paid more.

A promotion may also be a trap if it's moving you in a direction that is less and less aligned with the work you want to do.

One client shared,

"I am on a trajectory where I will be doing more and more of the parts of my job that are the least satisfying."

Another told me,

"I've recently realized that a lot of the core tasks of my job that become more important as you advance are my least favorite parts of it."

This client confidently chose to decline the promotion at her company because she could see that it was going to be more work that was out of alignment with her strengths. It may have made "no logical sense" to turn it down, but it was the right decision for her.

IT'S OK TO HAVE A BORING JOB
(IF IT WORKS FOR YOU)

The most controversy I've ever created on the internet was based on a blog post titled "It's OK to Have a Boring Job."

It caught the eye of a *Business Insider* journalist and long story short an article was written about this topic and the reaction was incredibly polarized. Some people were so incredibly relieved, and others could not fathom that I was giving people permission to have a boring job.

I don't think I've ever heard anyone say that it's OK to have a boring job. It definitely doesn't work for everyone. And it definitely does work for some people.

(If this concept blows your mind and sets you free, message me at lindsay@alifeofoptions.com. I would *love* to hear about it.)

It was early in my business when I noticed how revolutionary this message seemed to be. I'd been sharing it more and more often and after one particular workshop, participants kept coming up to me afterward saying how grateful they were to hear someone say that it was OK to have a boring job. So now I'm on a mission to tell people that it's OK to have a boring job if it works for them.

Here's a common experience for a lot of clients I work with: there's someone in their life that is encouraging them to change jobs because the job isn't fulfilling or challenging them. Or the client is feeling pressure from the expectations we put on our jobs to be fulfilling, challenging, well-paid, exciting, impactful, fun, inspiring, mission-driven... and the list goes on.

I uncovered the idea of a "Good Enough Job" a few years ago, after reading *Refuse to Choose* by Barbara Sher.[14] She describes the "Good Enough Job" as:

"If a job isn't unpleasant, doesn't eat up more than 40 hours a week, pays well, and provides security—it can give you the freedom to do all the things you love on your own time. People complain about unfulfilling jobs until they understand what the Good Enough Job actually is, and then they feel very different about them.

Think of it: a job that doesn't bother you, whose only crime is that it's just not enough to fulfill your life. But it provides money and security and the freedom to fulfill your life in your free hours. That sounds like a great job to me."

When I share this definition with my clients, one of two responses occur. One is incredible relief that their job doesn't have to be everything to them, and the other is "Do. Not. Want." (For some clients their revulsion to this concept is so

---

[14] www.barbarasher.com

strong that they start vigorously shaking their head before I'm even done reading the definition. It's immediately clear to them that 40 hours a week is too many to spend on something they're not excited about.)

For the latter group of people, that's a great thing to know about yourself. Your work is going to be one of the main sources of passion, drive, and purpose in your life and you should look for that. For the former group of people, that's also a great thing to know about yourself and you get to stay in your "Good Enough Job" without feeling the pressure of society or friends and family to make a move. As long as you're getting to choose the tradeoffs and know why it works for you, that's a great outcome.

As one client told me:

"The biggest "discovery" (I like to think of it as self-affirmation) was confirming to myself that meaningful work is an important value to me. I have tried to care less about work or only view work as a means to an end, but how I spend 40+ hours of my week is important to me."

This client recently discovered that, for her, a boring job is OK, and it doesn't mean she's a slacker or unambitious. It really allows her to spend time with her niece which is one of the most important parts of her life right now. I've had clients discover so many upsides of a boring job because it left them with a surplus of time or mental energy.

One client used his boring job to write a novel. He was responsible for tracking his own output and results and he found that he could get all the work he needed to get done in less than an eight-hour day. The rest of the day he worked on writing the novel he's always wanted to write.

Another client used her boring job to dedicate time and energy to her love of languages. She was able to clock out at a reasonable time every day and head to Russian class.

Yet another client dedicated her extra time and energy to volunteering for a crisis hotline. She was considering grief counseling as a future career and wanted to test it out before spending time and money on a degree and a complete career switch.

If it works for you and your life, a boring job can be just what you need. And that does not automatically mean that you are lazy, checked out, or taking advantage of your company. You can absolutely do a boring job incredibly well while showing up with integrity. All it means is that you're not relying on your job to fulfill your entire life and provide all of your challenges and excitement. It's one piece of the puzzle.

Now just because this works for you doesn't mean your friends and family will understand. One of the most interesting calls I've ever had with a potential client was with a guy who didn't want my coaching. He agreed to do an introductory call with me to get his friends and family off his back. They saw his unfulfilling job and were really pushing him to move to a job that was more fulfilling. He was perfectly OK with his unfulfilling job because he was excited to launch a new business and his boring job gave him the time and energy to do that.

Your friends and family really may be concerned that you're not challenging yourself in your job. The way to make a decision separate from their concerns is to be very clear about why your boring job works for you and why you're choosing it.

You can also re-evaluate at different stages of life. Just because you choose a boring job at this stage of life doesn't mean that you won't want to challenge yourself more in your job in the future, or vice versa. Your purpose can come from your family, your work, your hobbies, or your volunteering, and it may change several times over the course of your life.

My entire message is that you should do what works for YOU. Own that boring job if it works for you. Find a job that fulfills your drive and purpose if that works for you. Move between them as often as it works for you.

A boring job does not work for everyone, and the trick is to figure out if it does work for you. If it's revolutionary to hear that it's OK for you to have a boring job, I'll tell you again, so it starts to sink in.

It's OK for you to have a boring job if it works for you. The key is knowing whether it works for you.

EMBRACE YOUR "AFFIRMATIVE NO"

I recently came across Jeanne Safer's concept of the "Affirmative No" which she defines as "the refusal to pursue a course of action that, on serious reflection, you discover is not right for you". Safer created this concept in the context of deciding not to have kids.[15] As you can imagine, it immediately resonated with me and the work that I do.

She goes on to say that asserting an Affirmative No means "rejecting attitudes and courses of action [...] that most people treat as gospel" and "saying yes to points of view that may be unpopular but are in fact authentically in line with your own thoughts and feelings."

She writes that "any decision made in this way is not an act of rebellion; it is an act of willed self-assertion, of standing your ground on your own behalf" and that in order to "claim the benefits that come from advocating for the person you truly are as opposed to the one you think you're supposed to be, you must face your own reality no matter how it feels or what its implications may be."

---

[15] *Selfish, Shallow, and Self-Absorbed: Sixteen Writers on the Decision Not to Have Kids* by Jeanne Safer.

Oh my goodness, what an absolutely beautiful concept! If I could apply it to my worldview, I would create the conditions for people to give themselves the following permission.

If a "Good Enough Job" is not right for you, say no to it.

If it's not right for you, say no to a more demanding job, no matter how insistently your friends or family think that you shouldn't be OK with a boring job.

If the promotion is not right for you, say no to it.

If it's not right for you, say no to the idea that your passion, purpose, and drive have to come from your job, no matter how much the culture tells you it should.

DEEPLY UNSEXY RESULTS

In a world full of dream jobs, rocket ships, unicorns and hearing, "Quit and do your passion," I am promising none of that.

What I *can* help you achieve is incredibly life-changing and yet it looks so mundane to the outside viewer. And you know why that is? It has nothing to do with them. But it has everything to do with what is important to *you*.

I want you to learn that **what you want, matters**.

And you deserve to do what's right for you, as much as you possibly can.

3. Dear Goodness, the Pressure

Before we build our framework for clear and confident decisions, we have to start with a conversation about pressure. Because if we don't talk about it now, it's just going to pop up in all of the rest of our conversations and all of the exercises you'll complete by the end of this book. There is *so much* pressure about what we should do in our careers, what our careers should mean to us, where we should want to work, etc. We don't talk about it enough.

Here's the thing I hate most about career pressure.

You can't win.

If you stay at a company too long, you're called a lifer.
If you leave a company too soon, you're a job-hopper.

You're either stagnant or flaky. Awesome!

While we're here, who gets to define stagnant or "lifer"? What about all the interesting opportunities people get to have through internal mobility? And what about the people who want to stay in an environment that's a great fit for their needs? And what if people don't actually want recruiters reaching out to them constantly and asking to poach them? Calling people lifers is fear-mongering and causes people who may be very happy in their careers to second-guess themselves. Unacceptable.

Here's another reason you can't win. Spoiler alert, **the pressure never goes away**. It changes based on where you are in your career and sneakily shifts to fit whatever people think you should be doing at that phase.

For one client in his late 60s, the message was clear—it's time to slow down. "Why don't you just take your retirement and stop thinking so much about work?" he was asked. He felt like everyone around him was starting to phase him out mentally and it would have been easy to follow the expected path, but that wasn't the vision he saw for his next phase. He wanted to continue finding meaningful ways to contribute his youthful energy and lifelong perspective and it was incredibly inspiring to watch him do just that throughout our time together.

If I could please make a public service announcement before we move on:

Please stop telling people they've stayed in their job too long.

Please stop telling people they should retire when they reach a certain age.

Please stop telling people what they should do if you don't know what's right for them.

And maybe we can have a world where more people get to do what's right for them.

WHAT'S YOUR FLAVOR?

Everybody has an opinion about what you should be doing. Your family. Society. Even your own internal voice of self-doubt. It's so important to identify your own unique flavors of career pressure because everyone may be navigating something different. The more you can identify the pressures that you feel, the more you can separate those pressures from what you *actually* want.

Take a moment to reflect on the following prompts and questions.

The voices around me are saying:

I should be a...

I have to...

My career has to...

What internal pressure do you feel about your career?

What external pressure do you feel about your career?

What impact does that pressure have on you?

And what would be possible if you could relieve that pressure?

One client came to me with a lot of doubt about her ability to follow through and commit to one career path. She was frustrated with the path that she had been pursuing and wanted to explore other options. As we progressed through each exercise, all the results pointed to her current career path being a really fantastic fit and she regained a huge amount of confidence in the path she had originally chosen. She didn't realize how much family pressure was impacting her sense of value and confidence in her innate abilities and with that awareness, she created a new vision and deeper understanding of herself professionally.

You may also relate to a common finding that my clients feel more internal pressure than external pressure. They can't identify a person that is actively telling them that they should be doing XYZ but that somewhere along the line the message got lodged internally and is rattling around in their internal dialogue. If you had a similar experience, the good news is that you get to change your internal dialogue, but the hard part is also that we can be incredibly cruel to ourselves in our minds. It's another great moment to add lots of kindness and compassion as you navigate the pressure.

FORGET ABOUT THESE?

Once you've made your own list, I want to mention a few flavors of career pressure I hear quite often, in case any of these didn't make it onto your initial list.

The Noise

This is one of my favorite concepts from the book *Roadmap: The Get-It-Together Guide for Figuring Out What to Do with Your Life* by the creators of Roadtrip Nation (Nathan Gebhard, Mike Marriner, and Brian McAllister)[16]. He describes the noise as "the whirling cacophony of voices, advice, and expectations that drowns out our individual expression". This pressure can come from friends, family, colleagues, or what is considered culturally appropriate based on your family or culture.

Self-Inflicted Pressure

This can look like perfectionism, the expectations you place on yourself, self-doubt, the expectations you have for your job to be everything in your life, and more.

---

[16] roadtripnation.com

Passion

Passion is an interesting one. It's not that I am against you having passion in your work but the way that we talked about today often creates this pressure that you should only have one passion, it should be fulfilled at work, and you should probably know what it is by now. The truth is, not everybody is going to have their passion, purpose, meaning, and drive come from work. That will work for some people *and* we need to normalize that some people find their passion, purpose, meaning, and drive outside of work.

Systems of Oppression

We've talked about the many systems of oppression baked into the foundations of the workplace that make it incredibly difficult or impossible for many people to do what's right for them. How are you personally impacted? What pressures do you feel based on your race, age, sexual orientation, religion, or gender? Are you constantly "the only" in every room you're in whether that's the only woman, the only transgender person, the only Black woman, the only person with disabilities, etc? Are you trying to experience "freedom from the stereotypes of an Angry Black Woman, Feisty Latina, or Docile Asian," as Minda Harts says in her book *Right Within: How to Heal from Racial Trauma in the Workplace*[17]?

---

[17] https://www.mindaharts.com/rightwithin

PRESSURES BINGO

Another aspect of the pressure that I hate with a fiery passion is that it so often feels like a lonely and unique experience. Most of my clients feel that they're the only ones that feel this pressure and can't figure it out.

It's very bewildering to me when I talk to people all day every day and they're saying the same thing. How exactly does every person I talk to feel like they're the only one who doesn't have it figured out and everyone else around them knows what to do? (And where are these people who seem to have it all figured out?!)

I decided early on in my business that part of my role would be to collect all the secrets people tell me about the lonely pressures they feel and share them as much as possible to help everyone feel less alone.

I'd like to introduce you to the game I play called Pressures Bingo.

I'm going to share with you the top 10 pressures that I have heard over and over… and over and over again for years and you are going to compare them to your list of pressures to see how they compare.

1. It's too late to make a change.
2. I have to be constantly advancing in my career. Each role should be more impressive and more Senior.
3. My job has to be saving the world.
4. My job is my identity and it defines me.
5. I should be farther ahead in my career given my age.
6. I have to keep doing what I'm doing so I'm not giving up after putting in all these years.
7. I feel so behind and everyone else has it figured out.
8. My job has to be impressive and "cool" to other people.
9. I should have it figured out by now.
10. I should be able to figure this out on my own.

Wowza, that's a lot of pressure.

A recent client laughed when she looked at the list because it became so clear how absurd it is that we never talk about these things. We assume that everyone else isn't talking about it because they have it figured out but consider that we may just not be talking about it because it's not safe or the "thing" that people do.

So how did you do?

Do you feel none of these?
Do you feel all of these?
Somewhere in between?
Has it shifted throughout different phases of your career?

And if you're a manager or a company leader, which of these pressures are going unspoken in your workplace? How can you shine a light on the pressures your employees might be feeling?

Whatever you discovered, I hope this helps you see that you are not alone. You're a human being swimming in the pressure-filled societal soup that we're all in and it is Not. Just. You. These are the crushing messages we're constantly bombarded with. (And there's nothing to fix about you).

Now before we move on, we need to take a closer look at two of my least favorite pressures on this list.

"WELL, I'M NOT SAVING THE WORLD"

One of the biggest reasons that people waffle about making a change is missing a sense of contribution in their role. Here's what it has sounded like to a few of my clients:

"What is important for me to do in this world before I go, and what are the strengths that I want to contribute toward that important thing?"

"I feel quite sad that I'm not realizing the potential I have. I'm wasting precious time on this earth with wasted energy that I could be contributing."

"Now my pressure centers around the question of what am I doing with my life? What do I want to spend my time doing? This constant

questioning of life's big questions and feeling inadequate has me feeling overwhelmed and frozen."

Contribution is something that's incredibly important to many of us, but when I ask my clients more about the impact they're having in their work, I often hear an insidious phrase sneak in.

"Well, I'm not saving the world or anything."

Wait, what? What a strange response that we've been taught to give. We've been led to believe that we're either saving the world (in a very narrowly defined way) or we're doing nothing to be proud of.

I'm sorry, who gets to say what type of work is "saving the world?" What if *you* got to define what it looked like to contribute to the world in your own unique way? What if we each got to say whether work was our contribution to the world or whether we choose to contribute in other ways?

I challenged one particular client to look at what she actually wanted and what a meaningful contribution would look like. Her response was "earning money and producing something I feel good about."

"Saving the world" is filled with pressure and ambiguity, "producing something I feel good about" got to be tied to her values.

For another client, her response was, "I don't need to be saving the world, but I want my work to have a fast and direct impact on the consumer."

"Saving the world" automatically makes us feel like we're not living up to it; but "a fast and direct impact on the customer" is something she could start looking for that day.

If this hits home for you, what if you remove any disclaimer or assessment as to whether your work is "saving the world" and create your own definition of the contribution you want to make in your work or your life? Either you'll relieve some of the pressure you currently feel about your existing job or you'll know exactly what you're looking for in the next move.

"I SHOULD HAVE IT FIGURED OUT BY NOW"

I'll be honest: I hate this pressure.

It's one of my least favorite yet incredibly persistent pressures that basically exists as a catch-all for all other pressures. It's outrageously sneaky because it seems so simple yet can include comparing yourself to others, needing to have achieved something big, using an external definition of success, etc. The mean voice doesn't even have to use any creativity! It just pushes this one button and knows that it'll completely take you out. You'll be in an existential crisis and downward spiral in no time!

"I should have it figured out by now." *Blegh.*

It fills me with rage how many people have been taught this and how many societal expectations and double standards there are around how people get to show up and who gets grace for not having it all together.

What does it even look like to have it figured out, and who decided that was the goal? Society doesn't encourage us to share that we don't have it figured out. We're conditioned to share the shiny, polished, externally pleasing version at all costs and it's not safe for a lot of folks to not have it all together.

WHAT IF IT ISN'T ABOUT HAVING IT ALL "FIGURED OUT?"

Before we consider this question, let's look at what it would look like if we did have it "figured out" based on the nebulous expectations we place on ourselves.

If you knew what was going to happen every day for the rest of your life, where would the serendipity, spontaneity, inspiration, room for growth, and adventure be? What happens if you get to different phases of your life and you're a slightly different person with different needs and desires?

Something doesn't add up for me in this world of having it "figured out." It feels like a false end state where we have no more worries or questions about our purpose and contribution.

So, what might we aim for if the point isn't to have it figured out?

I would put the focus on exploration, experience, discovering as you go, being open to possibility, and knowing that there's never an endpoint where you feel like you know exactly what you're doing. It's about having a compass that helps you evaluate the different choices along the way and makes sure you feel good with every decision. It's embracing a lifelong exploration of who you are and what's important to you.

The next time the mean voice exerts absolutely no creativity whatsoever and pokes your "I should have it figured out by now" button, what belief would you like to hold instead?

WHAT WOULD YOU CHOOSE?

Now that we've covered all the different kinds of pressure you might feel about your work, let's create some new possibilities. If you could let some of these pressures go, what would you *choose* to believe about work?

Here are some of the answers I've heard over the years:

My job is one part of my identity and where I find fulfillment.

I get to try multiple things across my career and give myself the option to change my mind.

I'm on a lifelong exploration of finding meaning and purpose in my work.

It's OK to be doing OK.

I'm right where I need to be.

Phew. Feel that sigh of relief?

I invite you to start finding the voices that give you relief and freedom, and please, can we stop perpetuating the idea that everyone else has it figured out.

ACTION OUTSIDE OF PRESSURE

A beautiful thing starts to happen when we're able to notice the pressure and act outside of it.

One client quickly discovered how she expected her job to be *everything* to her. She saw the huge expectations she was placing on her job and how it had been creating tunnel vision around her.

My job has to be everything! It has to be sexy and make me look good to others! It has to provide all of my fulfillment!

She's been passing up opportunities because she's labeled them "boring" based on other people's expectations. She saw that she's really been limiting herself and with this new clarity, she immediately saw new options opening up.

And I'll never forget a somewhat surreal experience I had a few years ago where on two days back-to-back, two clients were set free by completely opposite realizations.

One client almost whispered her realization to me since it was still so new for her. She said,

"You know what I realized,"

"I'm not career-driven... and that's OK."

It was important to her to enjoy her work and do well and align it with her strengths, but actually what was most important was having time and energy to volunteer at her son's school.

The other client discovered the complete opposite. She made peace with the fact that she is career-driven, even though loved ones around her don't operate that way and she often compared herself to their outlook on work. She felt the freedom in choosing her own preference and started taking action in that direction.

It was such a stark reminder of how important it is to discover what's right for you.

4. This is Bigger Than "Quit or Don't Quit"

If you're on the fence about leaving your company, I want to widen your perspective from "Do I quit or not quit?" and give you many more options than you think you might have.

When you've been in a job for several years or invested decades in one company, considering a career change is a huge choice. You may feel like the decision should be easier to figure out, but there's so much more that goes into it than just 'is it time for me to move on'. I want to make sure you can see and acknowledge all of the incredibly difficult pieces that may be going into this decision so you can be incredibly kind to yourself about any of these areas that show up for you.

THANK GOODNESS YOU'RE RISK-AVERSE

I'm tired of the negative connotation of "risk-averse" and I would like to propose a rebrand.

So many clients share that they're risk-averse with a sense of sadness, shame, or I-wish-I-was-more-adventure-essness. They'll have that same sadness when expressing their desire to make a safe choice, like not quitting their job so they can keep their financial stability.

I'm tired of the weird pressure that exists to be adventurous, ready to leap at any moment, committed to quitting and going without a paycheck, living on the edge, being bold and risky—whatever it is. I would like for you not to beat yourself up for doing the things that keep you and your family stable, honor your values and your mental health, and work for your unique situation.

Instead of sadly wondering if you're taking the safe option, I invite you to ask yourself if you're taking the option that feels personally aligned and choosing based on your needs.

I recently had a call with someone who reached out to me and was interested in working together. On the call, she was convinced that she shouldn't make a change in her role even though things didn't feel good. She said,

"I've grown accustomed to my salary and benefits and I really worry about the impracticality of chucking it all for something new that I might not like."

My answer to that sentiment is always, **Yes, I agree!**

I absolutely don't want you to make a move if you don't know why it's the right fit for you. Honestly, I'm glad you're risk-averse, I want you to take into account your salary and benefits, and let's *not* take a big leap without de-risking the process as much as possible. In my world, we get to be crystal clear on *why* making the change is the right fit for you. I hate that we glorify "quit and do your passion" or just take the leap without doing the work to know if it's going to work for you.

I also want to focus on this piece, "I have grown accustomed to my salary and benefits." I think this is a really important thing to be clear about, because financial stability is incredibly important. In the society and world that we're in, money is important. We need it to make sure that we are safe, we need it to pay our bills, we need it to support our immediate and extended families, etc. So, we always want this to be a factor in any change we make, but you may not have noticed a sneaky little automatic assumption that pops in.

We tend to assume that if you make a change, you automatically will not be able to get the same salary and benefits. Now, if you are making a really big change, it's possible that you're going to have to take a little bit of a salary cut and that the benefits might be a little bit different, but I don't want you to automatically assume that if you make any kind of change, it is going to cut your salary and benefits. My clients often change jobs and get more money than they were making previously. So yes, there may be a situation where you may need to take a pay cut, but you get to choose that with intention and go into it knowing that that is a trade-off that you are choosing. And let's not forget that it could be better than what you have now, whether that's a higher salary or has benefits that are even more meaningful and aligned with what matters to you.

So, honor your aversion to unnecessary risk and make choices that honor you and your needs.

THE TERROR OF LEAVING A SEEMINGLY PERFECT JOB

Another reason this decision can be incredibly difficult is that you may be terrified to leave a seemingly perfect job for fear of what other people will think. It's entirely possible that people in your life have explicitly told you one of the following (or variations on a theme):

You're out of your mind to be giving this up.

Why would you ever leave this job, it's the best there is!

People would do anything to be at this company.

I've had so many conversations with people who have fancy jobs that look incredible on paper, have a great salary, don't even ask them to work too hard in some cases, and look like success to the outside world... but aren't what the person wants.

Something is missing, whether it's purpose, contribution, flexibility to focus less of their life on work, or something they can't put their finger on yet.

They've all known that it's not the right fit but they worry that they'll appear ungrateful if they leave the job. That they'll crumble under the backlash they get from other people questioning their decision.

And then the inner voices kick in.

Who am I to leave a job that's so great?

Why can't I just be satisfied in a job that everyone else thinks is awesome?

Do I really think there's something better out there?

Being able to make a decision that goes against what other people think, and knowing why it's the right decision for you, is one of the most empowering things you can do. People in your life may have the best intentions when giving you advice, but they don't necessarily know what's right for you.

I spoke to a woman who experienced the worst time of her life working at Facebook but felt she couldn't tell her family that she wanted to leave because they were SO proud of her for achieving what looked like the pinnacle of success.

I spoke to a man who worked at a prestigious law firm who was terrified to step away and leave the prestige despite knowing it was a terrible environment that he desperately wanted to escape from.

I am the person who voluntarily left Google and received many confused stares as to why I would ever leave the number one place in the world to work.

We get trapped in an external version of success and it creates so much dissonance in our lives. In some ways, the choice is to risk appearing ungrateful and have people judge you or be miserable at a place that doesn't work for you. The easiest way to make a decision you feel good about is to know *why* you're making the decision.

The clearer you are about what's important to you, what you want out of work, what energizes and drains you, what environment you need in order to thrive, and what your strengths are, the more clearly you'll be able to articulate that to others.

You'll know your exact reasons when you're asked the question "why would you ever leave XYZ job?" and if you choose to, you can confidently explain why it's the right decision for you (though you don't owe anyone an explanation). You can pinpoint that this value is missing, that strength isn't being engaged, what's actually important to me is this, I thrive in this type of environment, etc.

There is courage and leadership and grace in being able to do something that is right for YOU, regardless of what the norm is. Stepping through the terror and leaving the seemingly perfect job may actually be an inspiration for those around you. We don't know what kind of external versions of success those around us are trapped in.

If you're feeling guilty, ungrateful, or like you have a high bar for thinking about leaving a seemingly perfect job because you want more, I see you as none of those things. I see you as courageous, filled with integrity, and on the edge of potentially making one of the most empowering choices of your career. If leaving ends up being the right fit for you, thank you for being brave and showing us the way of doing what's right for you, regardless of what other people think.

WHAT IF YOU DIDN'T HAVE TO QUIT?

Before I get you too convinced that quitting is the right next step for you (as most of my clients believe when they land on my doorstep), let me share one of the most fascinating outcomes that continually blows my mind.

All of the pressure you feel has a silent undertone that maybe it's time for you to quit, but I think that we don't focus enough on the question of whether you can re-engage and re-invest in a place that has obviously been a fit for a good number of years.

It continually amazes me that over 50 percent of people who work with me don't quit.

More than 50 percent!

Yes, sometimes quitting is absolutely the right next step for someone, but more often than not, people quit because they have no idea what they want. When it's not clear what you want, quitting can seem like the only choice you have.

What's even wilder is how quickly this can happen and with zero external circumstances changing. The person's job and circumstances might look exactly the same from an outside perspective but what has shifted is their mindset and their understanding of what this job means to them, how it aligns with their strengths, the expectations they place on their job, etc. Or something does change and they find absolutely incredible opportunities in a different part of the organization, taking advantage of their company's internal mobility.

Now, I always like to be incredibly clear that quitting *is* the right thing for some people. If you are in a situation that feels unsafe to you, leaving as soon as possible may be the right thing. If you know that your mental health requires you to exit a situation, do so. If you know that you will be better equipped to answer the question of what's right for you if you leave this job, by all means, do what is right for you. But if that's not your situation, and you have the feeling that quitting is your only option, keep reading.

With a bit of effort, you have the power to change how you relate to your job— even if none of your external circumstances change. Often this happens by shifting your mindset, gaining perspective, or by understanding your strengths better.

PEOPLE CHOOSE TO STAY FOR ALL KINDS OF REASONS

"I surprised myself by quickly changing my current work situation and not only making it tolerable but actually fun and fulfilling."

When people choose to stay, it's not that everything becomes amazing and perfect (because we don't sugarcoat things around here), but there are many reasons that people make that choice. Sometimes they do fall back in love with their work and discover that it's a great fit for their strengths and values. Sometimes they don't have the luxury of being without a paycheck or making a big career move at this phase of life. Sometimes they know it's right for them to stay in the short term as a stepping stone to their next move. But the important part is getting to have a choice and understanding

WHY their choice works for them. The agency makes all the difference.

My client said it well:

"I was able to change my current work situation from 'I'm going to rage quit by the end of the week' to 'I'm looking forward to working on this project tomorrow.' The difference is really night and day, and has affected my home life where my husband and kids have even mentioned the attitude change."

One client was feeling bored, disengaged, and undervalued at his small company. His role wasn't a particularly good fit for his strengths, and he didn't have as much responsibility as he wanted. Through exploring his interests, he proposed a change to his manager to take on more work related to the company's finances. Despite feeling that he didn't have the formal training necessary, this was an area where he wanted to grow. Based on that conversation, he started down a path that led him to take over all financial aspects of the company. Just a few years later he was reporting to the CFO.

Another client had no energy or motivation, and it was spilling over into her personal life. She discovered that she's had a lifelong dream of becoming a concept artist and decided to start taking steps to move in that direction. She created a 6-month plan that allowed her to stay in her current role for great financial stability while building her portfolio. She focused on gaining the skills necessary to eventually make the jump.

A third client came to me concerned that her job wasn't challenging her at all. Her family and friends kept commenting that she could do better. After clarifying her values, it became clear that although the job was less challenging, it was allowing her to fulfill her biggest value. Providing for her family was her number one priority. This job allowed her to do that and she was willing to accept the tradeoff of less challenge at that point in her life. She started seeing her job in a completely new light.

You may also choose to stay in a job because of something outside of the day-to-day work. You may choose to stay somewhere that has the disability accommodations you need to thrive or you may need health insurance coverage that is transgender-inclusive. You get to choose any reason to stay in a job.

Before you decide that you absolutely need a career change, let me invite you to add some compassion to all the pressures you're feeling and give yourself the space to explore safe steps you can take to find what's truly right for you.

DECIDE WITH CONFIDENCE

As I said before, I have no attachment to whether you quit or don't quit. My sole commitment is that you get to make the choice that works for you and decide with confidence.

Here is what it sounds like to move on with confidence:

"I feel way less trapped in my current situation because I'm confident **the best choice for me is to leave it.** *I feel comfort in knowing that the problem is not me or my failure, but that the environment has really become a terrible fit for what I need to thrive. I feel less distracted by the drama and more focused on moving on to the next thing."*

"I am totally free of the burden or illusion it would be best for me to stay in my current job."

"Thank you for your help in discerning a job with this new company last year. It has been an exciting year, and I have thrived at this company. **There are great things around the corner.** *Thank you again. I truly feel much more fit for this job than as a traditional attorney and feel better about my career than I have ever felt."*

And this is what it sounds like to reinvest with confidence:

"Just a couple days after last we spoke, **I made the decision to stay at my current job** *and take the promotion, and I have felt very good about that decision ever since."*

"Today I was officially transferred to the Data org at my company to start a new position starting March 1st! While I'm not sure that this will be a long-term permanent shift in my career **it's certainly the next step for me.***"*

"I have gone from feeling burnt out, isolated, working mainly on projects and with people who didn't jive with my beliefs, to working on a project I have dreamed of doing for years, outside, with people who energize me, and I got a promotion in the process!"

But before you make the choice, I'll take you through the process that gets clients incredible clarity and confidence in their decisions.

5. Trust the Process

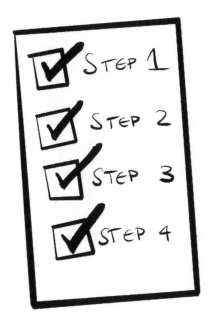

When I was trying to decide for myself whether it was time to leave Google after 6 years, I cobbled together every exercise I could find to help me make a decision I knew I'd be happy with. That framework morphed into the one I use with clients today and the framework I'm overjoyed to share with you in this book.

You're here because you also love frameworks (*swoon*) so let the structure do its job. Do the exercises, create the framework, and be open to all kinds of outcomes. Some parts may be difficult along the way but trust that things are happening just as they should. You are never stuck, you get to explore, and you will always have options.

In order to get the most out of this process, I want to share my worldview and some agreements that will help you along the way.

Let go of "doing it right." As soon as you start doing some of the exercises that follow, you may fall into the trap of "Am I doing this right?!?" Let me reassure you that you don't need to worry about that here. It's not about having it "figured out," there's no "wrong" way to follow the framework, and it's a pesky lie that everyone else has it all figured out and you're the only one who's struggling. As long as you show up curious, open, and willing to trust that it will work for you, you'll discover the answers you need.

Complacency is not what we are after. The fact that you're here means that you're not looking for a life of "it's fine," you're looking for a life of "this feels right for me." You want more for yourself and here we honor your desires. Release any thoughts of "I should be happy with what I have..." while you are secretly wanting more for your life. You're playing for an awesome life.

Do what's right for you. Your well-being is the most important thing in this process. If anything doesn't feel right or you're banging your head against a wall with any part of the framework, adjust or move as needed. You know best what's right for you.

Play full out. You know you have one precious life, and you have a lot you want to contribute. Play full out while following the framework and get connected with your desires and the contribution you want to make in the world—whether it's through your work or not. You can have as many careers as you want and it's never too late to make a change. You're on a lifelong exploration of figuring out what makes you feel most alive. Don't rush it. This process is about having the courage to do what's right for you and honor your choices (and it's never about sexy results that other people will think are cool).

You get to have fun. Let me say that again. *You get to have fun in this process.* I know that dealing with this challenge has most likely been draining for years, if not decades, and I'm here to bring a bit of levity and hope. Yes, you'll work hard but it'll feel much harder if you take yourself too seriously. Let's add fun and playfulness to your exploration and see if you can enjoy the adventure along the way.

Always add more kindness, compassion, and grace. This is often the hardest one for people to agree to! But all I need you to do is to be open to adding more kindness, compassion, and grace for yourself in this process. I'll remind you as many times as I possibly can, and if you're lucky, by the end of this process you'll have the "Kind Lindsay" voice in your

65

head that many of my clients tell me about. Instead of using the exercises as an opportunity to beat yourself up (I bet you're already too good at that), use the information to add awareness and intention to your future actions. There's always a good reason why things haven't felt good and we're going to find the way to articulate it that allows you to be incredibly kind to yourself. When in doubt, add more kindness!

If you can agree to those, you're going to crush it and discover exactly how to do what's right for you.

YOU'RE CLOSER THAN YOU THINK

One more thing to keep in mind before we move on to revealing the framework.

What if I told you that you most likely already know all the answers to any question you're struggling with?

The one piece you're missing might just be a process to untangle your thoughts and desires from the external pressures you feel. Here's what a recent client discovered:

"Most of the time, you already know the answer to your questions but this process can help you to untangle all the thoughts. With clear thoughts and values, you can explain your motives and visions more clearly, which gives you confidence."

And I've noticed a very strange phenomenon that happens over and over again when I meet with clients. I take notes during my sessions so I can share their insights and findings from our discussion, and I often reflect back to them what I've written down.

More and more often clients say, "Oh can you share that incredible way you phrased that thought" or "I love when you came up with the idea that xyz..." but 100 percent of the time it was not me that came up with the wording or the idea. I am only the notetaker. You're the one saying the incredibly thoughtful, clear, and insightful thing and I'm just the one writing it down.

It's almost like we don't allow ourselves to hear our own clarity. I have to constantly (lovingly) correct people that no, it was not me that came up with that, that actually came from inside your being.

I love how this client put it:

"Throughout this process, I was surprised to learn that deep down I know my direction, have the voice to advocate for it, and the power to act on it. I need to utilize that confidence and power to direct my life. This process has rekindled the confidence I lost."

Or if you prefer another client's sentiment at the end of working together, *"News flash—you know yourself pretty well."*

I'm going to plant a seed of possibility that you already know what's right for you. I want you to trust that you aren't that far away from clarity and confidence. I want you to trust that you can discover your desires and find where your power is.

And this process is going to do just that.

A SPECIAL NOTE FOR MANAGERS

If you're reading this book as a manager, not only do I hope that you get to become clear and confident about your choices, but that you pass this gift along to your team. Remember that your reports are most likely feeling guilty and ashamed that they can't answer your questions about what they want.

I see my job as equipping both you and your report for the clearest conversation of your relationship so far. When your report gets clear about what they need in their role, you are better equipped to help them get into the right place, like this client:

"I talked to my director about taking on new responsibilities, and have been working on more interesting work since then, and am happier in my job!"

You will now have an opportunity to lead from a place that is clear and decided and to be an incredible role model and help others get there too.

A SPECIAL NOTE FOR HR AND COMPANY LEADERS

If you're reading this book as an HR leader or someone who is concerned with retention, I want to equip you with the most effective way to retain and engage the people who are the right fit for your company (both for you and for them).

Instead of seeing money, raises, bonuses, title change, perks, etc. as the main (often costly) levers you have to retain your people, what if I told you that I retain people without all that? I retain your people by getting them clear about their strengths, values, etc., and molding their roles to be in alignment with those things.

To be clear, I'm not saying that money has no effect, and please *do* pay your people well, but if someone has no idea what they want, money is not going to make a difference in the long term. They may stick around for a few months, but the issue of not knowing what would make them happy will rear its ugly head soon enough. If you're truly committed to keeping your people and getting them into the right fit for them, help them to have a great conversation about what they want using the tools in this book.

Here's the power of getting people clear about what's right for them.

They can identify areas of their job they enjoy and make changes in that direction:

"Things at work have been going as good as I can ever remember in my working life. Thanks for helping me identify some of these things I enjoy doing and making changes at my job."

"I see my job, my company, and my opportunities completely differently now. For the first time, I feel like I can say I enjoy aspects of my work and can focus on them as much as possible."

They can shift the perspective of their existing role:

"I didn't know my strengths the way I do now, so I thought I had the 'wrong' job. Now I've discovered that my job allows me to engage in most of the activities that bring me energy and aligns nicely with a number of my strengths."

"I've been able to make many changes at my current job, mainly in how I'm showing up energetically and approaching my work. I can now see the value in my job and have stopped the negative running commentary which has made a huge difference in my day-to-day satisfaction."

"With these learnings, I have a new sense of purpose and motivation to go out and achieve the big things I've had in mind for years. Now I feel so much excitement and clarity about where I'm going and who I am."

They can communicate where they want to go and take advantage of the awesome internal mobility you've created:

"I feel a lot more empowered and in control of my own career. In discussions that I had this week, even, I noted that I was a lot more comfortable talking to people about where I want my career to go."

"I gained a clearer vocabulary for talking about my strengths in the workplace and my needs as a worker. This is improving my confidence."

And my favorite outcome is when they release the pressure they feel to have their job be absolutely everything to them:

"I feel more at peace. While my job isn't perfect there is so much about it that aligns with the life I want for myself."

That is what retention looks like when it is filled with integrity and care for the employee. They are choosing to stay because it's right for them, not because of a promise of a raise or promotion. I invite you to get curious about what would truly make it worth it for your folks to stay and if you discover that the company is not a good fit for them, support them in getting into a place that is.

MY HOPE FOR YOU

Remember how my purpose in this world has nothing to do with the specifics of your job or career? Neither does my greatest hope for you out of following this framework. My greatest hope for you is this client's experience.

"I feel like myself again."

When you have been struggling with feeling stuck in your career for months or years, it's very common to have lost your spark. You're not showing up at work the way you want to, and you just don't feel like yourself. This happens when you're in environments that are misaligned with your strengths and values. When you're constantly waffling about what to do to make your situation better. When you're feeling overcome by the pressures and expectations that the world has for you.

My greatest hope is that you'll be able to return to who you truly know yourself to be.

"I feel like myself again—hopeful, optimistic, and excited about the future. It is a night and day difference. Each set of exercises built my confidence and prompted me to look at things in a completely new way. I was able to make connections that I couldn't see before. Working with you has given me tools to come back to and a fresh new way to approach my entire life with more kindness, curiosity, and playfulness."

The world will still be designed in a way that most likely doesn't make it easy to be yourself. But it'll be easier to find your agency when you feel like yourself again.

As part of my program, I have clients reflect on their growth over the three months with me to see just how far they've come. I love that the reflections are often so simple, yet profound. It goes back to my commitment to providing clients with deeply unsexy results—it doesn't look flashy in a way that your friends will be impressed, but my goodness it will feel more meaningful to you than you could have imagined. Here's a recent example:

"When I first started, I…" was full of self-doubt/negative self-criticism, lost when articulating values and strengths, stuck in inaction, and fearful of change/reaching out for help.

"Now I…" can easily articulate what matters to me, what I bring to the table, and what I want from a career. I am more confident that I am making the best decisions for me.

There's such a beautiful feeling of calm, clarity, confidence, and self-assurance. It's so grounded.

"I'm making the best decisions for me."

That's the whole goal. Not the flashy quitting. Not the impressive promotion. Not the life that looks good to everyone else. You making the best decisions and doing what is right for you.

And now it's finally framework time! I couldn't be more excited.

PART 2

MAKE A DECISION

Right For YOU

One of the sneakiest questions that plague many people I work with is:

"If I say this is what I want in a job, and then I get it, will I actually be satisfied?"

It's actually a great question to ask (and gets to the core of the work I do) but you can also feel its heaviness. It shows a loss of confidence, a lack of trust in your own decisions, and a deep desire to know what is right for you.

This is such a common experience. You've spent so much of your time listening to external pressures, going after shiny things, wanting to look good to others, and measuring yourself on external definitions of success. It's especially prevalent if you've been burned by your past decisions, been let go, or moved around a lot. It creates a serious lack of confidence that you actually know what's right for you.

What allows people to come back from that? Relieving external pressures, honing in on core values, and being able to articulate why something wasn't a good fit. And it can happen faster than you think.

So now that we've reframed and structured much of your thinking (aka given you *way* more reasons to be kind to yourself!), we can focus on rebuilding your trust in your own decision-making. The second part of the book is all about building your own Framework of Freedom to make the decision that works for you. This will allow you to finally be DECIDED so you can move forward with your work and life.

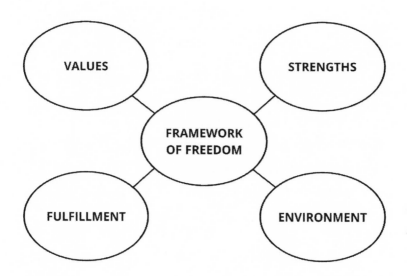

I'll take you through the four components I've found to be most helpful for making a decision that is right for you. You might find some of the questions and exercises difficult! I always joke with my clients that I did not promise them easy, I promised them unshakeable confidence in their decisions and that is what I will deliver. But be kind to yourself along the way and as always, do the parts of this process that work for you.

ARTICULATE YOUR OPTIONS

There's one other task for you to complete before we jump into building the framework. I want you to articulate the decision you're waffling about and make a list of all the potential options that are swimming around in your head. This can range from the time-sensitive and tangible (a promotion you need to accept or decline by next week), to the hypothetical (you've always thought about going back to school for creative writing), to the escape hatch (why can't I just become a potter in the woods?!).

We want to capture it *all* so that you feel like no stone is left unturned in this process. Towards the end of the book, we'll be able to assess all of these options and cut down any of them that actually aren't right for you.

6. Framework Component #1: What Do You Value?

Values help us answer the questions, *what is important to me in life* and *how does work fit into that?*

Oftentimes people feel like they somewhat know their values and have given them some thought, but there's something incredibly clarifying that happens when people really sit down and take the time to intentionally write them out.

There are many ways to discover your core values. I personally love using a data-driven approach to how you've made decisions in your life so far to see what we can learn about what you value.

I want you to grab a piece of paper and split it into two columns. In the left column, I want you to make a list of life decisions that you have experienced so far, across work and life. They can be decisions such as choosing your college or university, choosing not to go to college or university, moving somewhere new, deciding to take or leave a job, spending a year traveling, coming home to take care of family, etc. What matters is that it's a list of decisions that feel meaningful to you.

Once you have the list of life decisions in the left column, in the right column I want you to write down the motivation behind each decision. What were you craving more of when you made that decision? What were you moving away from? What about that situation did not work for you? What were you excited to have more of in your life by making that decision? Example motivations might be that you weren't feeling challenged, you craved adventure, you wanted to be closer to your community, or the status quo was costing you your health. Highlight the values that fueled the decision-making and don't put any values down that you think *should* be on the list.

It's possible that already at this point in the exercise, you've learned something about yourself. In almost every one of my workshops, I do this exercise, and some participants find that it's difficult to even identify decisions that they have been able to make in their lives. Sometimes their family dictated their decisions or they didn't feel like they had a lot of choice in the matter for other reasons. You know the drill, but I will lovingly remind you, please add lots of kindness, compassion, and grace for yourself if that's the case. Take it in as awareness of how much of your life decisions have felt out of your control and use it to add intention to future decisions.

The results can also be jarring in another way, like when a recent client noticed that they'd spent 40 years without an intentional awareness of their guiding principles. In this scenario, it can be very easy to take the default route of beating yourself up about past decisions or the lack of awareness. If you're able to shift into kindness, we then get to ask the question, what do the next 40 years get to look like with incredible awareness and intention around my guiding principles? How can I start living the life I want and doing the work that fulfills me? There's an incredible opportunity to start making different choices today.

ARE YOU MY VALUE?

Once you've created your list of motivations, I want you to circle any words that look like values. In my example, I would choose Challenge, Adventure, Community, and Health. Other values might be Financial Stability, Growth, Integrity, Connection, Beauty, and Independence.

You may already see themes that have shown up across many of your decisions. I want you to put all of your values in a roughly prioritized list and see how they feel.

Do these feel like the values you choose to make decisions going forward?

Are there values in this list that were handed down to you, but you no longer choose?

Are there values that didn't show up in your decision-making but that you wish to be as part of your framework for decision-making going forward?

The good news is that you get to ultimately choose your list of values and how you make decisions. And if it's not feeling quite right, know that this is the first attempt and you can always come back and add or edit as needed. Values often are a work in progress and can shift at different phases of your life, so you don't need to feel that this is your final list of values for the rest of your life. See if you can capture what feels important to you at this phase of your life.

DEFINE IT FOR YOURSELF

Creating a list of values is where most other values exercises stop, but this is just the beginning of getting to understand your values. The most important part that most other exercises miss is to define these values for yourself.

Framework Component #1

If I asked 100 people for their definition of Growth, I would get 100 different answers. This partly explains why you can feel so unfulfilled in your role because you may be craving Growth in a particular way and yet your manager or leadership team is focused on creating Growth based on a completely different definition.

Same with Recognition or Appreciation. Your manager might be recognizing or appreciating you in a certain way that does not match your definition and the way that you like to be recognized. In their eyes, they're doing everything they can to recognize you, and in your eyes, it's doing nothing to fulfill your need for Recognition. So, it's incredibly important for you to understand your definition of your values, not only for your own decision-making but to also be able to communicate that effectively to the people around you.

Defining your values for yourself creates clarity, confidence, and freedom in your actions.

So how do you define each of your values in a way that is meaningful to you? One way is to start with the phrase:

To me, [value] means...

Here are a few examples of how that's allowed clients to define their values in ways that are meaningful to them:

> ➤ To me, **Stability** means that I have a foundation and safe space so I can be comfortable thinking about goals for my life.
> ➤ To me, **Friendship** is understanding and being understood by people I care about.
> ➤ To me, **Adventure** means I get to try something I haven't seen, done, or experienced before (a new food, a new city, a new hobby).
> ➤ To me, **Community** is feeling like I am a part of something bigger than myself; that I feel connected to the people around me, and that I am contributing in some way to a shared purpose or goal.
> ➤ To me, **Financial Security** means being able to pay my expenses, have investments for later in life, not have to worry about day-to-day wants, and live without fear of running out of money.

I hope that by clearly defining each of your values for yourself, your final list of values feels more tailored and meaningful as you use it to make decisions that are right for you.

STABILITY? HRMPH.

I need to take just a moment and acknowledge something that often comes up with the values exercise. If you found Stability popping up on your list of values, you may have… feelings about that. Clients often struggle with this value as it can feel constricting, unadventurous, boring, uninspiring, or any number of descriptors that people don't like. They don't want Stability to be one of their values.

But here's the importance of defining it for yourself. When I asked one of my clients to let go of any negative connotation of Stability and truly define it in the way it showed up in their decision-making, this beautiful definition emerged.

"Stability means feeling safe enough to take a chance."

Can you feel how expansive and supportive that definition is? It's such an incredible way to honor your wiring. Does it mean you're boring and unadventurous? Does it mean you're stuck in your ways? No and no. It honors your desire for financial security, safety for your family, a good job, or whatever it is for you while allowing for the safety to take a chance.

For each of your values, you get to create the definition that allows ease and freedom for you and your life. And when you're feeling negative or stuck about a value, see if you're setting yourself up to fail by understanding a concept based on someone else's definition or the widely accepted negative connotation of the word. Define it for yourself to see where you can create freedom, creativity, and action.

DIGGING DEEPER

Now we get to get into the juicy questions about how our values are showing up in life and work and how they'll allow us to make decisions.

What stood out to you or was surprising about this exercise?

This is always a great first question to ask yourself in any of the exercises we'll be doing today because it surfaces insight that you may not have otherwise seen. Were you surprised at how often Adventure showed up? Did you find it interesting that Health didn't show up as much as you expected it to? Do you notice that many of your decisions have been driven by Financial Stability but that you don't actually want it to be one of your main drivers?

Are all of your values fairly equal or is there a point where there's a drop-off of importance?

It's important to identify whether you would describe any of your values as non-negotiables or deal-breakers. It can be incredibly helpful to think of our values in different tiers to understand how important they are to us in any future decision we'll make. Your top three values might feel like non-negotiables to you, just your top value might be your deal-breaker, or your values may feel equally important to you. There is no right or wrong answer here, the important part is that you get to choose and articulate what feels right for you. This is the first part of the decision-making framework that we are building and any decision you make is going to be looked at through the lens of values. If you can say, I know that my top two values of Health and Growth are my non-negotiables then any decision that you consider or any opportunity that comes your way is going to need to clear the bar of those two values. If it doesn't, that is not the right opportunity for you and you can say a calm, thank you but this is not the right fit for me. You do not need to spend any more of your time and energy considering that opportunity if it's not fulfilling your values in the way that works for you. On the flip side, if the opportunity seems to honor and prioritize Health and Growth, you can continue the conversation with confidence.

For one of my clients, she was conflicted about her software engineering job when she was told that as she moved up at the company, she would be able to work from home less and less. During our work together she realized that flexibility and being able to spend time with her young daughter were two of her most important values and that she really wanted a career to support that. After exploring a variety of options, she ultimately took a position that not only was 100 percent work from home but also promoted her to Senior Software Engineer. This was a huge accomplishment because she felt it was an empowered choice that honored her two non-negotiables, while getting incredible validation and a confidence boost.

How many of the values are being prioritized in your current role?

It's so easy to forget this step but it's one of my favorites because it's so immediately clarifying.

Take the list of values that you've just created and see how well these values are being prioritized in your current role. This will give us one lens to understand what is working and not working in your current situation.

Run through each of your values and record how well each one is being honored or prioritized in your current role.

Here's how I like to break it down:

Yes: This value is honored and prioritized in my role.
No: This value is not honored and prioritized in my role.
Meh: This value is somewhat honored in my role or this value is being honored but not in a way that is meaningful to me.

We can often forget the "Meh" category but it's so important to recognize if the value is there but not in a way that is meaningful to you! Your fulfillment will come from having your values show up at work in the way that you define them.

So how did you do? How many of your values are being honored and prioritized in your role and what does that illuminate about why things feel the way that they do? If your non-negotiable or deal-breaker values are not being honored and prioritized, that gives you a huge clue as to why things aren't feeling good. It also gives you a blueprint for making some changes.

One client noticed that Learning and Growth had taken a backseat and started brainstorming ways to take add learning to their day to day. Another client saw that Adventure was lacking and looked for opportunities to find something new to experience, learn about, and immerse themselves in.

How could you experiment with honoring and prioritizing your top values in your role? If you have Tier 2 values that aren't currently being honored and prioritized, how might you bring those more into your work? Start to get curious about how your values can start to show up in your work now that you have clarity about what is important to you.

If you discovered that none of your values are showing up in ways that feel meaningful to you, I want to give you two ways to think about that finding. Predictably I will first suggest kindness and compassion for what that brings up, and then I invite you to see it as a confirmation of why things are feeling the way that they are. There is always a logical reason why we don't feel good in our roles and you have been able to uncover one of those reasons. I hope it helps you start to rebuild the trust in yourself (no wonder I'm feeling this way!) and articulate why you're unhappy. I will also encourage you to see it as an incredible opportunity.

We're at 0 values fulfilled right now. What does it look like if *one* of your values is fulfilled in a way it feels great to you? What if you get to have *three values* fulfilled in ways that feel awesome to you? And what could it look like in the future to feel like *most if not all* of your values were really firing on all cylinders? I can't promise that we'll go from 0 to 100 in one step, but I want you to see how much possibility there is for you to feel better in your work as you bring in more and more values. You can only go up from here!

No matter what you found with this question, whether 0 of your values are fulfilled or all of your values are fulfilled, there is no inherently right answer. If 0 of your values are fulfilled, it doesn't automatically mean that quitting is the right thing for you. If all of your values are fulfilled, it doesn't automatically mean that staying is the right thing for you. You can make any choice, for any reason, as long as you know why it works for you. You can choose any tradeoffs you like, as long as you're choosing with intention, and it doesn't have to make sense to anyone else. I don't want you to worry that any of the findings in these exercises are going to mean that you have to quit or have to stay. You always get a choice with how to interpret what you discover.

Which of your values show up at work and which of your values show up in life?

Some of my clients feel a distinct separation between work and life and different values will show up in different spheres. For example, I had two clients with Growth as one of their top values. One client said to me, I absolutely need to feel growth in my work otherwise I feel stagnant and drained. The other client said, I actually don't need growth in my work as long as I feel like I have 10/10 growth in my personal life which looks like taking piano lessons and writing a novel I'm working on. Take a look at your list of values and see where you would like for them to show up.

If you're someone who feels that work and life blend for you and it doesn't feel as compartmentalized, awesome! You know you're going to be looking for work that fulfills as many of your values as possible.

As I will continue to say, there is no right answer but the clearer you can be about how to interpret your values (what they mean to you, their importance, and where you want them to be honored), the easier it will be to make decisions and cultivate opportunities that are right for you.

EVALUATING NEXT STEPS

Now comes the real fun! We get to use this very first part of the framework to test out all those ideas you came up with for potential next steps. For each of the ideas you had, list them out and do the Yes/No/Meh check.

Does the internal move you're exploring seem like a great fit through the lens of your values?

Is your "escape hatch" actually a terrible fit that you can lovingly check off your list for good?

Do you have questions about how the role at the new company would prioritize your non-negotiables and need to learn more?

Awesome. It's all about articulating what feels good to you and *why*, along with knowing where you need to get more information to make the decision that is right for you. Confidently cross off anything that doesn't feel aligned and excitedly give your time and attention to anything that feels like a great opportunity. And that's only using one piece of the framework! We've got many more to go to fully create a tailored framework for a lifetime of confident decisions.

7. Framework Component #2: What Dimensions of Work Are Most Important for Your Fulfillment?

As I mentioned earlier one of the biggest things you might be struggling with is being able to articulate what's working and not working about your current role. We now have the lens of values to help articulate your current fulfillment and this next exercise will give us even more of an understanding of how things are going currently and what dimensions of your work are most important to you.

This is a standard coaching tool often called The Wheel of Life, originally attributed to Paul J. Meyer[18] and it's a simple yet effective way to check in with how things are going. You can use it as a tool to assess how things are going in life and you can also use it as a tool to assess how things are going in your career. For our purposes, we're going to look at your fulfillment in eight different areas of your career, adapted from Co-Active Coaching's Professional Assessment Wheel[19].

Grab another sheet of paper, draw a big circle, and split it into eight pieces like a pizza. If you've been missing arts and crafts in your life, this is the time to break out the markers, the colored pencils, and the glitter pens because remember that we get to have fun in this process.

Once you've drawn your circle (or maybe it's more of an oval, not a problem), label each of the eight slices with the following areas of your career. If any of these dimensions do not resonate or are not part of what makes up a fulfilling career for you, choose categories that do.

> Recognition
> Climate and Culture

---

[18] https://pauljmeyer.com/the-legacy/industry-pioneer/
[19] https://coactive.com/co-active-coaching-toolkit-resources/

> ➢ Generating Results
> ➢ Creative Self-Expression
> ➢ Career Development
> ➢ Communication
> ➢ Relationships
> ➢ Personal Well-Being

Once you have your pieces labeled, I want you to go around the circle and rank your fulfillment in your current role, at this moment, on this day, in each of these areas. You'll use a scale from 0 to 10 where 0 is not at all fulfilled in this area and 10 is highly fulfilled in this area. And the aim is not for everything to be at 10 as fulfillment and balance are going to look different for everyone.

Now, I've been facilitating this exercise for years and I'm going to invite you to do it pretty quickly to really tap into your gut reaction. I know that if I give you too long you may start overthinking and second-guessing your answers. Give yourself 30 seconds or so to move around the circle and rank each dimension from 0 to 10. It'll look something like this:

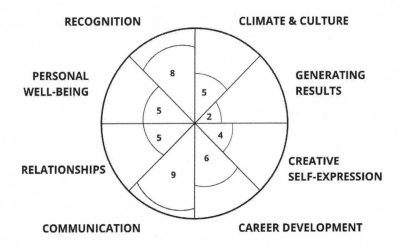

Now you can go back and jot down a few notes on why you gave each of the areas the ranking that you did.

So now you have a visual representation of how things are feeling today, in this moment. You may find that you have one of three reactions:

1. Oh no, my job is even worse than I expected and there are many areas that are lower than I'd like.
2. Oh wow, when I zoom out and look at all these areas, I actually feel better about my role than expected.
3. Yep, this is pretty much what I expected to see, some ups and some downs.

Whatever your reaction, on either side of that spectrum, I invite you to take the information in as data, to be kind and compassionate about what you discovered, and to use the results to make intentional choices about what comes next.

The way we implement the results of this exercise is to take any area that feels lower than you'd like and think about the actions you could take to increase the score by 0.5. If it's a 3, what would move it to a 3.5? We are not trying to get it to a 10, we are not trying to fix everything right away, and we are not trying to take huge action and overwhelm ourselves. We are actually looking for the tiniest actions that would make an impact for you in that area because it's so easy to overlook the small experiments you can run.

Here are a few ideas from previous clients to get you thinking:

If you want to increase your score in Relationships, reach out to one new person a week to get to know them.

If you want to increase your Communication score, proactively prepare an agenda for each 1:1 with your manager.

If you want to increase your score in Recognition, one of the easiest things is to take time to celebrate your own accomplishments!

And if you want to increase your score in Generating Results, block off strategy time each week.

Now you get to brainstorm a few 0.5 actions you could take to increase any of the scores that are lower than you'd like. We're looking for experiments we can start running this week or next to see what's going to make a difference.

HYPERFOCUSED ON THE DOWNSIDES

This exercise is so simple, yet I've seen it have a huge impact on so many clients. I never know when it's going to affect someone in this way but I love getting to witness it.

There are two clients in particular that I'm thinking of. The first one came to me convinced that she needed to quit her job. Not only did she want to quit her job, but she wanted to leave her company, her field, everything. Burn it all down. She was trying to figure out, do I go right to business school or do I make another kind of change?

We did this exercise in our second session together and it helped her zoom out and get a bird's eye view of how things were going across many of the different areas of her job. Within the hour, she laughed and had this incredible realization: wait a minute, I actually really like my job. It's really just these couple of things that if I could tweak or do more of, that would actually make a big difference for me. I've been so hyper focused on these two areas that are missing. She discovered her 0.5 activity and started asking for more opportunities to present to stakeholders (which was one of her favorite activities). She became known as the go-to person for presentations to stakeholders and she's still in that job years later, with three promotions since I've known her.

The second client did this exercise and by the following session, she had a completely different outlook on the company she'd been in for 15+ years. She felt like herself again, hopeful and optimistic, and she saw that the job was perfect for what she needed at that phase of her life. I asked her what she thought made all the difference in this exercise and she said that it gave her agency to make change (even small ones that made a big difference) and it allowed her to let go of beating herself about her job and replace it with kindness. She also started taking more initiative in these dimensions of her work instead of waiting for opportunities and relieved a lot of the expectations that she placed on her job.

The 180-degree shift is an incredible thing to witness and it's more common than you think. Sometimes we really do get hyper focused on the downsides of our job and it's hard to see the overall picture. It's crucial to zoom out and understand whether the desire to quit is the right thing for you or if there's a chance to re-invest in your current role with intentional and meaningful tweaks.

(If you do this exercise and have this outcome, I would love for you to share it with me by emailing me at lindsay@alifeofoptions. com. I'm so excited to hear more stories of this epic shift!)

CREATIVE SELF-EXPRESSION

This area of fulfillment is often rated incredibly low by many of my clients because they're convinced that they're in a profession that doesn't allow for creative self-expression. Here's the thing I need you to understand. Creative self-expression is not automatically built into any job or field and if you expect it to be built in, you'll most likely be disappointed. The trick with creative self-expression is to design it into your current role, in small or big ways, that are meaningful to you.

I remember one client saying,

"Lindsay, I'm a lawyer, there's zero creativity in my job."

You may also feel that way about your field. But when he started looking for tiny 0.5 ways to add creative self-expression, he said, you know what would make a difference, adding a little bit of wit to the emails I send to my colleagues. That small change made him feel like more of himself at work.

Give yourself the freedom to discover what creative self-expression could look like in a job without needing it to be built in by default. You also get to reflect on how the environment feels safe or unsafe to express who you are. If it doesn't feel safe to fully express who you are, it may not be somewhere where you choose to stay. Or you may choose to express the level that feels right to you. It's not the same level of ease or safety for everyone to feel like themselves at work, so you always want to look for what's right for you and where you have agency to be yourself.

THE UNCOMFORTABLE QUESTION

Now that we have an idea of how things are going in your job, I have an uncomfortable question I need to ask you.

Where are *you* contributing to the environment that you hate?

I ask you this to help you identify your locus of control and to take responsibility for how you're showing up at work. It's very common that when we feel stuck or unhappy at work, we're not actually showing up as the person we want to be. How do I know? Remember how I mentioned I hit rock bottom? Well this is how a 1:1 with my manager started:

"I'm getting feedback that you're checked out and have no motivation."

I still wince when I think back on that moment. It's not at all how I see myself and the way that I want to show up in the world. I never want to be the person with a bad attitude, showing up checked out, and getting called out by my manager, but the reality was that I was that person. It was how I was showing up. It doesn't feel good and if you're similarly showing up in ways that you're not proud of, I know you don't want to be showing up that way either.

When I ask clients where they're contributing to the environment that they hate, it often gets quiet as they really take a look.

Yeahhh… I'm participating in office gossip, which I really hate.

I am absolutely showing up to meetings checked out and playing on my computer.

Oh, I definitely have a bad attitude.

This isn't to make yourself bad or wrong or to give you any more reasons to beat yourself up. I want you to start noticing and interrupting those patterns. Where do you have control over your behavior and how you're showing up that would ultimately make a big difference if you could shift it? Have you made all the effort that you can to feel more fulfilled in your role?

Here's what it sounds like to explore creating new possibilities:

I notice how much I've been making things worse for myself with my mindset. I've been coasting along pretty unhappily but now I'm getting curious about what I have control over.

I do actually have a reasonable amount of flexibility, how can I practice adding something enjoyable every day?

My energy is drained when I continue to beat myself up about not being engaged and not doing a good job. I'm going to notice those thoughts and plant new ones as my 0.5 actions, like "I'm finding more ways to re-engage every day in my job and my life, in my current role and in the future."

It's also important to be clear when circumstances are outside of your control. It would be dangerous to think that it's always on you to survive and fix an environment that doesn't work for you. You get to balance what is in your control and what is out of control and ultimately decide whether it's the right thing to exit a situation.

So there you have it, another part of the framework to be able to make a decision and move forward with your life. I hope it illuminated the dimensions of work that are most important to you, so that you can mold your current role to be an even better fit or prioritize those aspects in your next move. This is also a great tool to use on a monthly or quarterly basis so you can always feel proactive about your work fulfillment and pinpoint what's out of alignment to make adjustments.

8. Framework Component #3: What Strengths Do You Want to Contribute?

"*W*hy did it take me until I was 40 to know what my strengths are?!*" a client asked me last year.

I have no good answer to that question and unfortunately, it's all too common. It's possible that you did a strength assessment at some point in your career but if you're like me, it kind of went in one ear and out the other. The information was overwhelming or it was way too easy to say *yeah, yeah, yeah but isn't this how everyone works? These things are so easy; everyone can do this.*

(ATTENTION: Any time you have the feeling that "Oh this ole thing, isn't this how everyone works" that is an immediate indicator that the thing you're describing is actually an incredible strength of yours. More on that in a moment.)

Whatever age you happen to be at this moment, let's make sure that you know what your strengths are as quickly as possible. I don't want you to go another year without knowing what you want your contribution to be.

UNCOVER YOUR STRENGTHS

As with values, there are many different ways to uncover your strengths. Depending on your preference you may choose to take an assessment that will give you an idea of what your strengths might be, or you can spend some time thinking about the work that you love doing and the things that come naturally to you and create your own list of strengths. As always, you do what's right for you around here.

If you are on team "please let the robots help me discover my strengths," there are two assessments I can recommend. As a Gallup Certified Strength Coach, I am clearly biased and use the CliftonStrengths talent assessment with all of my clients. Now, remember that I am an engineer, so I have a healthy skepticism of all of the assessments out there. I have chosen to use the CliftonStrengths assessment for years because I continued to see it having an incredible impact on people, both at Google and with my clients. You can uncover your top five talent themes within the CliftonStrengths model[20]. The other assessment that I used during my coaching certification is called the VIA Character Strengths Survey which is free[21].

If you choose to take an assessment rather than create your own list of strengths, I have an additional question for you that I want you to answer before we move on. I want you to look and see, what was your first reaction to the strengths that the assessment delivered? I always like to tell my clients that these are robots designed to tell you who you are and so we always take the information with a grain of salt. You get to intentionally choose what is helpful about the output and what you choose to release from the output. Our first reactions can often be incredibly helpful in discerning what we agree and disagree with.

I had a client describe it to me this way. The output that they received from their CliftonStrengths assessment was kind of like a friend offering to draw a portrait of you. You sit for the portrait and when they're done, they turn the drawing around and you get to see what their perspective is.

Oh, wow. Is that how you see me?

That's such an interesting way to capture who I am.

I would never have seen myself in that way, huh!

---

[20] https://store.gallup.com/p/en-us/10108/top-5-cliftonstrengths

[21] www.viacharacter.org

It's an opportunity to reflect on somebody else's experience of you and see if there are any areas where you want to plant a seed of opportunity for your identity. You might think, "Hmm, the robot believes that I have incredible strength in this area, even though I don't necessarily see myself that way. If I try that new possibility on, what evidence might I find that I do have strengths in that area?"

There's a beautiful potential to expand the appreciation you have for yourself and the unique gifts that you bring.

NOW WHAT?

However you came to your list of strengths, let's start to learn how to apply them to your current role. I'll take you through the series of questions that I like to ask my clients.

Which of these strengths, if any, are being used in your current role?

You knew this one was coming!

Let's use the same framework of Yes/No/Meh. Right away you'll get a sense of how many strengths are being used in your role and whether they're showing up in ways that feel good to you. As before, what you discover here can affirm why things are feeling the way that they are feeling and also gives you a blueprint for where you can start to take action to bring more of your strengths into your role.

Many clients find that zero of their strengths are being used in rewarding and meaningful ways and it immediately affirms why they're feeling the way they do. Others find that all of them are engaged, like my client at a small startup where she got to build both the team and strategy, engaging her relationship building and strategic thinking strengths. For another client, she was using her problem-solving skills but in isolation, rather than with a team.

Which of your strengths do you use most often at work? Which of your strengths do you wish you could use more often?

I love this pair of questions because they bring awareness to the current situation and uncover your desire for how you would like it to be. Because you've been lacking awareness about your strengths up until now, there likely hasn't been much thought given towards which strengths you would like to be using more often.

These questions can also help you see the connections between the work that you do or the field that you're in and how you might be able to use those strengths. Or it may uncover that there's a real misalignment between the field and the strengths that you want to contribute in your work. I'll remind you that these exercises are never an opportunity to beat yourself up but an opportunity to increase your awareness of what you want to create.

Where are you swimming upstream?

I've had many conversations with clients about the idea of swimming upstream.

You will likely show up with your strengths, no matter what environment you're placed in. You'll bring your positivity, your problem-solving, or your communication skills because that's who you are. The question you want to ask is, is this an environment that supports and appreciates those strengths, or do I continually feel as if I am swimming upstream, fighting against the culture or expectations of the organization. It may feel incredibly draining for you to be in an environment where you are bringing your beautiful strengths, but the work you're doing is not asking those strengths of you.

For which of your top strengths do you want to be known?

You probably have a default reputation at work as the person who is a great problem solver, gets things done, brings the team together, etc. And you might be great at those things, but what do you actually want to be known for?

One client wants to be known for the integrity of how she shows up and being able to genuinely relate to people. Another wants to be known for her analytical and relationship building strengths, being someone that people want to work with and is great at thinking things through and solving problems.

Which of your beautiful and unique strengths do you *choose* to be known for? And how would you start being known for that strength tomorrow?

UNIQUE VALUE

Remember when I mentioned that the thought, "But this thing is so easy!" is an immediate indication that it's an incredible strength of yours? Let's talk more about your unique value and my two favorite frameworks to discover what that might be.

Expected vs. Unexpected

I want you to fill in the following phrase:

Not only do I have [ABC strengths] that you might expect from someone in my role/field, but I *also* have [XYZ strengths] that may be unexpected for somebody in my role/field.

If you think about looking around your workplace and seeing everybody who does a similar role that you do, what is an inherent part of the job? And how do you stand out from everyone else who might have the same job title as you?

One example is how I learned to convey my unique value as a career coach. When I first started my business, I used to tell people how weird it was that I was an engineer (as you can imagine, I don't recommend that strategy) because I hadn't yet been able to see it as part of my unique value. Now I can see that

111

not only do I have many skills around empathy, curiosity, and relationship building that you would expect from a career coach, but I have strategic and analytical strengths from my engineering background that are quite unexpected as a coach (and therefore why I call myself a coach for analytically minded people).

What would your colleagues say?

Another way to practice discovering your unique value is to imagine the following scenario.

If I asked all of your favorite colleagues and managers from any of the previous jobs that you've held, what is it about you that made it *such* a pleasure to work with you, what do you think they'd say?

It's so natural for us to overlook the strengths that we have because they feel so easy to us and we assume that everyone else has the same experience. The people around you can often have a much greater appreciation for the unique ways that your brain works.

NARROW VIEW OF LEADERSHIP

We have a very narrow view of leadership in the U.S. Leaders are mostly white, mostly men, and tend to be celebrated for being loud, extroverted, risky, outspoken, commanding, or tough. Often when my clients find that their strengths fall outside of that narrow band, it's hard for them to see themselves as leaders. They may wish that they had more of the aforementioned traits and lament the strengths that they have.

But here's the way I see it.

What if the strengths that you have are exactly the leadership qualities we need?

Does the world need more of the leadership styles we already have? With the fires that are burning in all corners of our world, I would argue that the answer is no. We need a balance of all different kinds of leaders. We need to see a wider variety of leaders so that more people can feel that their strengths lend themselves to leadership.

Just because we mostly see male leaders, in my experience this narrow view of leadership also holds back men who want to lead in ways that fall outside the norm. I remember a conversation with a client who was worried about applying for a VP role at his company because he leads with relationship building strengths that thrive in interactions with individuals, rather than motivating and leading big groups. He had to look at how he could bring that strength to the VP role knowing that we almost never get to see leaders operate in this way and it was a huge opportunity to be a new kind of leader in his company.

Let's also acknowledge that women of color have a uniquely difficult time navigating leadership. Dr. Ciera Graham writes about 6 of the "dirty words" that are attributed specifically to women of color:

Ambitious. Opinionated. Direct. Controversial. Pushy. Sassy.

She goes on to say,

"Women leaders face what we call a double-blind bias, or a mismatch between what is expected of a leader and what is expected of a woman. [...] This has even more disastrous impacts for women of color, as they must navigate both racist and sexist assumptions about identity and leadership style. We have a long way to go before we can rid ourselves of these dirty words for women—but what makes me excited is seeing women who are owning their power, vigorously challenging racist and sexist assumptions about their identity, and unapologetically redefining women leadership."[22]

What would be your most authentic leadership style based on your unique strengths? Is it quiet, relationship-based, environmentally-focused, behind the scenes, or choosing to honor people over productivity?

At the end of working with one client, she declared,

---

[22] https://www.careercontessa.com/advice/name-calling/

"My values and those aspects of my personality that I always considered soft skills or not really related to work are actually unique strengths in the workplace that make me a strong employee and a leader in my own way."

I hope that you're able to expand your view of what constitutes leadership strengths so you can see yourself as a leader and make room for others around you as well.

NEW POSSIBILITIES

It starts getting incredibly exciting when clients find totally new ways to use, embrace, and own their strengths. For one client she was initially convinced that she needed to leave the field of engineering she had been in for decades, but when we uncovered her strengths, it was clear that teaching and training was a huge area for potential. She ended up transferring internally to a role that trains engineers which she never would have previously considered.

Another client discovered that her top strength was Input and in the CliftonStrengths model, people who lead with Input are described as having a need to collect and archive and they may accumulate information, ideas, artifacts, or even relationships. This client was a consultant and initially, she had no idea how Input showed up in her work or how she could consider using more of her top strength. Once she started looking for ways that Input showed up in her work it became clear that it was one of the main reasons why her best clients appreciated and loved working with her. They always came to her to get thoughtful recommendations and by leaning into her strength even further, she started developing even more resources to help clients understand new issues that were important to them. Is it possible that your biggest strength is part of the reason that clients and coworkers love working with you?

For a client who spent 20+ years at his company, he felt like a big fish in a small pond and wondered, am I as great as I think I am? He was worried that he wouldn't be marketable anywhere else, but this strengths exercise lit an incredible spark in the possibilities he saw possible for himself. After taking the assessment, he sent me an email that said,

"Buckle up! I am fired up this week! CliftonStrengths nailed me and I am incredibly energized by the results."

He had a completely different energy and sense of confidence for the remainder of our time together because it became abundantly clear to him that he had a lot to offer.

Another example that always comes to mind is a client who discovered through this process that she had a lot of coaching, mentoring, and relationship-building skills. It surprised her to learn that she might be a good fit for a career she had briefly considered—grief counseling. Throughout our time together, she started following that desire and took a lot of focused action. Several years later, she let me know that she had completely transitioned into being a full-time grief counselor.

Here's a summary of what I hope that articulating your strengths will make possible for you.

I want you to be able to appreciate the unique value that you bring.

I want you to be able to embrace and own the strengths that come naturally to you.

I want you to be exposed to a wider set of possibilities than you previously saw for yourself.

I want you to be able to discover your authentic leadership style, *especially* if it looks different from the default.

And I want you to be able to decide how your strengths get to show up in your work and life.

9. Framework Component #4: What Conditions Allow You to Thrive?

So much of your success depends on the environment that you're in. In order to complete the framework, we're going to learn everything we can about your prior roles and create a definitive list of what you need out of your environment in order to thrive.

My favorite way to do this is an adaptation of an exercise in the classic book *What Color Is Your Parachute*. It says:

"Plants that grow beautifully at sea level, often perish if they're taken ten thousand feet up the mountain. Likewise, we do our best work under certain conditions, but not under others. Thus, the question: 'What are your favorite working conditions?' actually is a question about 'Under what circumstances do you do your most effective work?' The best way to approach this is by starting with the things you disliked about all your previous jobs."[23]

A CATHARTIC LOOK BACK

It's time to grab another sheet of paper and split it into 4 columns. This exercise is one that clients often describe as being cathartic as they dive deep into understanding all of their previous roles within the new framework that we're building.

In the first column, make a list of all of the previous roles you've had/companies you've worked for.

In column 2, list the distasteful working conditions in each role. These are the conditions that contributed to decreased feelings of effectiveness, belonging, or fulfillment at work. This could be office drama, lack of interaction with the customer, or a distracting workplace with little sunlight.

In column 3, you'll want to flip those distasteful working conditions to articulate what *does* allow you to thrive at work.

---

[23] https://www.parachutebook.com/

What Color Is Your Parachute describes this as the keys to your effectiveness at work.

You believe your contribution, belonging, and fulfillment at work would be at a maximum if you were able to work in these conditions. You might thrive when there is office communication centered in integrity and respect, regular interaction with your customers, and a workplace that allows for quiet focus with plenty of sunlight.

In the fourth column, reflect on the 1-3 main takeaways from each job:

What did you learn about yourself?

What skills did you acquire?

What dealbreakers did you discover?

What stands out to you as you look back?

A few examples:

I need to know what will become of my work to know if it's purposeful.

I learned how to talk with patients and family members in an authentic, intimate way.

I discovered my absolute love for customer service.

BUCKETS

Take a deep breath and congratulate yourself for taking the time to truly examine your past jobs and learn everything you can from them.

The final step is to create a list of working conditions that you know you need in order to thrive. If you've found themes that started to emerge across all the different roles and companies, you can also break it down further into different buckets. Are there specific aspects to the day-to-day work? Are there conditions that relate to your manager/leadership? How about the culture of the company?

And once you have this glorious list of what YOU truly need to thrive, how many of them are being honored in your current role? Are there changes you can make to your day-to-day work? Is it clear that the leadership and culture at this company are incompatible?

Again, the more clearly you can articulate what you need in order to thrive, the more clearly you'll be able to communicate that to others and get yourself into work that fits.

NOTE FOR LEADERS

If you're reading this as a manager or a leader, how are you creating the environment for all of your employees to thrive?

Black Women Thriving 2022[24] is a ground-breaking report co-written by Ericka Hines, J.D. and Mako Fitts Ward, Ph.D and project of Every Level Leadership, that serves as both a guide and call to action.

The authors write, "We know that when Black women thrive, an organization will have broken free of so many unquestioned and inequitable norms and power structures that thriving will replace surviving for everyone."

I NEED TO CONFESS

I CAN'T WAIT ANY LONGER. I have to reveal to you that I've been playing a trick on you this whole time. Don't worry! It's the most loving trick I play on all my clients and it's quite delightful.

When clients first come to me, they often try to convince me that they're "all over the place" and that none of their actions so far make any sense. I respond very compassionately while not believing a word of it. I cannot believe that based on my experience over the past several years.

So, what is this trick that I've played on countless humans?

I've asked you to do a lot of exercises so far regarding values, areas of fulfillment, strengths, and working conditions. All

---

[24] everylevelleads.com/bwt/

very different questions, yes? But the trick is... it turns out, you are a deeply consistent human... and every exercise is going to have the same answer.

You are a deeply consistent human.
You are a deeply consistent human.
You are a deeply consistent human.

I love getting to tell people that they are a deeply consistent human. That their values make sense with their strengths that make sense with the environment they need that makes sense with the contribution they want to make... and so on.

There's something quietly revolutionary about this phrase. It cuts through the stories clients have about feeling out of control or impulsive about their choices so far, being unclear about what they want and who they are, and not being able to figure out what works for them. By the end of the program, they have a deep sense of knowing who they are and trusting the deep consistency of their being.

(And fun fact, I love saying this SO MUCH that I commissioned incredible artwork from Alison Hawkins[25] with this phrase).

---

[25] https://alisonhawkinsportfolio.com/

"BUT SURELY, I AM NOT A DEEPLY CONSISTENT HUMAN"

It may not be immediately obvious to you, but it's always easier for someone else to see it.

For one client with Relationships in their top values, they also discovered relationship-building strengths and working conditions that talk about the importance of your team and people-related activities.

For another client with Growth as their top value, the activities where they were doing repetitive stagnant work were draining and they wanted high scores in Career Development in the wheel exercise to feel like they were growing in their career.

Another client's deeply consistent humanity kept coming back to three things. Learning, Telling Stories, and Creating Impact.

Your version will look different, but the same themes will start to show up over and over again. There's something so calming about this phenomenon. I like to joke with my clients that my job is only complete when you are officially tired of how often you've seen the same results show up, confirming your deeply consistent humanity.

You want what you want! It all makes sense when you look at all the pieces together. And the sooner you can (1) allow yourself to want what you want and (2) start intentionally prioritizing those things, the sooner you are going to become unstoppable.

Go back and look for yourself. Where is your deeply consistent humanity showing? How do your values and working conditions overlap? The wheel and your strengths? Has it always been about people and problem-solving? Learning and sharing? Collaboration, storytelling, and results?

I invite you to consider that it's always been clear, you just haven't seen it this way before. And with clear knowing, there can now be confident decisions and effective communication.

10. The Framework of Freedom

I truly hope that you've already learned so much about what's right for you by examining all of these exercises, but if it's not crystal clear yet, do not fear. Now is the time to put it all together into your own tailored Framework of Freedom so you get to experience what I like to call the Easy Yes and the Easy No. When you're incredibly clear about what's important to you and what enables you to thrive in the workplace, it becomes the easiest checklist when assessing opportunities.

This opportunity doesn't honor my top two deal-breaker values? Easy No.

This opportunity honors my values and allows me to use all 5 of my top strengths? Easy Yes.

This recruiter is offering me jobs that don't fit with the environment that I know allows me to thrive? Easy No.

This opportunity hits enough of my requirements and I know the tradeoffs that I'm intentionally choosing? Easy Yes.

Even when it's more complicated and you're having to assess more nuanced aspects of a company, such as where they are with their commitment to anti-racism or whether they accommodate and support people with disabilities to thrive in their workplace, the clarity of what *you* need helps you find your agency.

A CALM CHOICE

It's so delightful to see a client make an incredibly confident choice for the first time. It often confuses them how incredibly calm and anti-climactic it feels.

For one client, a recruiter reached out to her to offer her a shiny tech job.

Before we worked together, this experience would send this client into a whirlwind of chaos.

Why don't I want this job? It sounds perfect on paper! Other people would love to have this job, who am I to turn this down?

And so on and so on...

In this case, it was a few weeks before our time together ended and the client responded with,

"Thank you, but that role isn't a good fit because of ABC. I'm actually looking for a role with XYZ characteristics, please let me know if you come across something that would be a good fit."

It was so beautifully boring and calm. It was missing all the waffling, the energy and focus suck, the existential crisis, the regret, getting derailed and distracted by things that don't matter, the second-guessing, and the having someone else try to convince you it's a great job for you.

Now?

No thanks, not a great fit. No need to spend my energy on it, and onto intentional uses of my energy and focus.

You calmly and confidently make a choice and then move on with your life.

Another client's manager was moving on from the company and he was offered the job. He immediately had a clear sense that the job was not for him and was able to quickly articulate why that was the case. He was delightfully confused in that moment at how quickly and calmly it happened. There was a sense of, *"Uhh, hold on, I just made a decision very calmly and easily, am I doing it? This is a weird and new experience..."*

When this happens for the first time, I get to acknowledge clients and welcome them into my special society of "people who make decisions they feel great about." It's anticlimactic and so deliciously boring on the outside. You waste zero of your precious energy and attention on things that don't fit. What a deeply unsexy moment to an external viewer but a deeply moving experience for the person making the decision.

Remember the escape hatch of burning it down and becoming a potter in the woods? That came from a client of mine and after dreaming about this (and honestly letting it distract her for years), the client laughed and saw that it was actually a terrible idea based on her framework. And just like that, she was able to close the door on that option knowing that it was the right choice for her.

ULTIMATE KINDNESS AND RESTORATION OF SELF-TRUST

Another beautiful outcome is truly seeing that your unhappiness at work is due to a misalignment of fit rather than a personal failure. My experience is that there is *always* a reason why something wasn't a good fit and the more language you have to articulate why something isn't a good fit, the less you beat yourself up.

Consider these beautiful realizations from two clients:

"This process did give me a good understanding of why I found present working conditions at the company where I worked so untenable and how caring a lot about what happens there isn't a failure, but a beautiful expression of my strengths and values. A look back also revealed how much more I thrived and was able to achieve in good or better working conditions."

"Through the program, I discovered my values and strengths, which clarified why I was struggling in the work environment I started in, and it wasn't because I was stupid or lazy, but because the situation wasn't a good fit for me."

The most powerful example of this was a client who came to me unemployed and feeling pretty lost. His last several jobs had started well but ended poorly, either with being let go or parting on bad terms, so his confidence was shaken and he was unsure if he'd ever be able to find somewhere he could fit long term. He also felt his background was all over the place and he had bounced between too many jobs to make any sense of it.

After examining his values, he was amazed at how consistent he had been with his decision-making despite the seemingly chaotic path. Over and over again, his decisions were made following his values of integrity, curiosity, and human

131

connection. He was able to connect consistent threads through all of his past experiences and understand why they weren't a good fit. Armed with this information, he landed a job that he stayed in for several years, ultimately rebuilding his confidence and his trust that he could find a job that fit.

I invite you to look for any places where you're beating yourself up and can shift into ultimate kindness by articulating what was out of alignment.

TAILORED FOR YOU

Let's put together the framework that allows you to calmly and confidently make a decision about your career that's right for you. There's no right way for the framework to look, you can create it in a spreadsheet, you can create a visual for yourself, or you can simply write it out. I recommend including the 4 components (values, dimensions of work fulfillment, strengths, and working conditions) along with anything else that you discovered about yourself along the way.

And then, you get to decide.

Looking at your framework, go through each component and assess how it aligns with all of the ideas you have about what could be next. (And if you'd like a template of the spreadsheet I use with my clients, you can access all the digital resources for the book at www.alifeofoptions.com/rightforyou)

How does each option stack up against your values? How well does each opportunity allow you to use the strengths you want to use more of?

Is it clear that even though this company has been great for a number of years, it's no longer a fit for what you need at this phase in life? Are you able to see your job in a new light and articulate where you can focus on improving to make it the right place for you?

And if you don't have every piece of the answer, that's ok too. Let the framework illuminate the areas where you need to gather more information so you can make a confident choice.

IDEAL JOB THOUGHT EXPERIMENT

Sometimes I ask clients to do this quick thought experiment so that they are 100 percent sure that it's time to stay or time to move on.

Based on everything that you have learned about yourself in this process, I want you to describe the most ideal job you can imagine at this company. Describe it in as much detail as possible and make sure you include everything that would make it a dream job.

Then, take a look at that job description and ask yourself,

If I was given that job tomorrow, would I want it?

And if the answer is yes, there may still be more to explore before you leave. You might be able to have a conversation with your manager or your leadership to share that vision, start learning about where that role may already exist in the company, or find where you have the agency to take the smallest actions towards that ideal. Of course, I can't promise that the ideal job exists or is possible, but this thought experiment does allow you to identify any last options to explore.

And if the answer is no, then you know that you have exhausted every possible option in this environment and the right thing for you is to move on.

Two clients had completely different experiences when they did this thought experiment. The first client wrote her most ideal job description and then had the realization that it was effectively the job that she currently had. Yes, there were some ways that she could lean more into the parts she enjoyed, but she actually had a lot of flexibility to create exactly those conditions from the role that she was in. The second client saw immediately that even if he could get that most ideal version of the job, he wasn't excited about it. The challenges he was facing were too entrenched in the leadership of the company and he really was ready for a new challenge and a new adventure.

IT DOESN'T STOP THERE

The main purpose of the framework you've built is to make a decision that you know you'll be happy with and that is right for you. But there are several other ways to use it as you start getting into action in your life.

Decide what jobs to apply for.

If you decide that the right thing for you is to move on and you're starting to apply for jobs, use your framework as a high bar. Do not apply for anything that you can already see will not be a fit for what you need as it will needlessly drain your energy.

I should also have a warning for employers that interview anyone that has gone through this process because you get to start asking incredibly clear and direct questions that truly matter to you. The job interview gets to be a two-way street where they are assessing you for fit, and you are assessing them for being a fit with what you know you need.

Start a new job with incredible intention.

The framework is awesome if you want to start a new job with incredible intention. How are you going to make sure that your values are honored and prioritized as you begin this role? What conversations do you want to have with your manager from the beginning so that they're able to help you thrive? After your first 30 days, what do you notice when you do the wheel exercise and what needs to be shifted for the next 30 days?

Have the best manager conversation of your life.

When you're clear, it's amazing what can happen in one conversation with a clear ask. Now, my rule with manager conversations is that you get to choose what feels safe to you and you don't need to share anything that you do not want to. I also recognize that people can be received differently when making direct asks in their work. It is always up to you whether a conversation with your manager feels right, but I want to share two positive experiences clients had with their managers due to the clarity of the communication.

"Even simply asking my boss for more collaborative work has paid off! He now has me joining meetings on a new technology innovation project. I was impressed with my boss and myself on real change coming from a simple ask."

"I used your prompts and dove into the conversation with my manager today and it was one of the best conversations I've ever had with her. We had so much to talk about and I think this is the start of a new level of understanding and connection between us."

Of course, it's not that you'll always get a yes or it'll always make a change, but the chance is *much* higher when you're making a clear request.

Proactively cultivate opportunities.

When you're able to share what you're looking for and what's right for you, you gain an incredible ability to proactively create opportunities for yourself. Whether that's saying that you're interested in learning more about Finance and then reporting to the CFO a few years later or asking for more opportunities to present to stakeholders and becoming the go-to person at your company for that task.

The more you share, the more you create.

RIGHT FOR YOU?

The right decision for one client was to pursue a new role at a company that was better aligned with her values.

The right decision for another client was to move to a new team within the same company where she could engage more of her strengths.

The right decision for another client was to go back to grad school, a lifelong dream.

They put together their tailored Framework of Freedom and made the decision that was right for them, knowing exactly why it was a fit.

So now it's your turn to build your framework and then let me ask you...

What decision is right for you?

And when you know the answer, I'm just going to drop this right here so I can be **so excited for you** and help you celebrate: lindsay@alifeofoptions.com.

MOVE FORWARD WITH YOUR CAREER (AND LIFE)

The results of going through this process are never the sexy things that look exciting to other people. They're deeply personal and meaningful outcomes that allow you to be more of who you are. I want to share a collection of the most beautiful reflections and results clients have experienced across the years. They most often show up across these seven areas:

A renewed version of me

I feel refreshed and refocused. I feel more prepared, more optimistic, confident in my abilities, and very hopeful. I'm really excited about being better equipped to describe my gifts and learn how to explore new career paths. I found a new excitement and positivity about my career and reclaimed bandwidth that was previously spent in unproductive spirals entertaining thoughts of job switching or comparing myself to others. I feel more expansive and open to life.

Clarity on what's important to me

I have a very clear idea of what my values and strengths are and what I'm looking for in my next job. I have my story clear how I got here, why I got here, and where I'm going next and why. I better understand what I need in my job to feel satisfied. To satisfy my values and strengths and let my skills shine, I've got to try something else.

Trust in myself and affirmation of my experience

I am a consistent human being and I see that my values have informed my decisions throughout my life. I am finally trusting my instinct and I'm seeking out a better fit for myself. I feel confident and trusting of my inner voices. Now I understand why I was so miserable. It wasn't my shortcomings that were the issue, it was the environment and circumstances I was in that didn't line up with my values and strengths, so I was set up to fail.

Showing up powerfully in my communication and my leadership

In my conversation with my manager, I used my new confidence to give a voice to what matters most to me. I can be more powerful in the role where I am. I surprised myself through this process by quickly changing my work situation and not only making it tolerable but actually fun and fulfilling. I've learned to ask for what I want and see that opportunities open for me when I ask for them. I've been able to make changes at my current job and how I'm showing up energetically and approaching my work. I've discovered the power I have to change how I think and perceive the situations I am in.

Focused, no longer distracted

I've learned to make clearer and faster decisions by learning to say no. I am unperturbed that there are bazillions of jobs out there I seemingly should want but don't. I've become a person who can clearly think through what things I'm not willing to compromise on which makes my decision-making much clearer and easier. I limit the energy I spend on unproductive thought patterns and what-if scenarios.

Empowered and in control of my career

I am more confident that I am making the best decisions for me. I feel empowered to make day-to-day choices to focus energy on what I want to do. I can use the agency I have to make choices that play to my strengths and values. I will embrace my new definitions of success and enforce the boundaries I need to feel balanced. I will continue the hard work of evaluating and reflecting on the progress I want to make in these areas and implement change when needed. I turned my bad work situation into a very positive situation and that opened even more opportunities for me within the company.

Decided and in action, no longer stuck

I feel way less trapped in my current situation because I'm confident the best choice for me is to leave it. I drastically changed the circumstances of my current role and it makes me feel accomplished and relatively happy at the end of the day. This process has allowed me to see how critical it is to start taking action and being aware enough to shift my mindset is a game-changer. I don't have the exact destination figured out but I have a pretty clear direction and plenty of ideas to explore. This is the lightest, most peaceful, and content I've felt in years, and I feel ready to conquer what's ahead of me."

I'm perpetually moved by the courage, vulnerability, and commitment to their lives that my clients show.

The courage it took for the VP of Finance to resist the outward pressure to be CFO, knowing that she didn't want that career progression.

The vulnerability it took for the engineer to acknowledge her negative attitude and choose to create a completely new outcome in her role.

The commitment to her one beautiful life it took for the lawyer to give herself space to try on being a writer.

I have no doubt that you've been able to do the same in this process. What would you add to this list to acknowledge and celebrate what you've discovered and who you've become?

A LIFETIME OF CONFIDENT DECISIONS

I always tell my clients that this process is a long-term investment.

Yes, we are working together because there is an acute challenge that we need to work through, and at the same time, we are building tools that will continue to support you for the rest of your career.

I can't stress enough that this feeling of clarity and confidence in your decisions is the way you now get to live your life. You have the tools to recreate this experience at any moment in the future when things don't feel right. Because it will happen! There will be moments where you start feeling the funk again, you're unsure whether it's time to make a move, or an opportunity drops in your lap that you have to assess. Pull out the values exercise, take a look at your strengths, and see where you're out of alignment and what changes you can make or how the new opportunity stacks up with what you need. You now have the resources to make a confident decision at every step of the way.

And I love when I hear from clients, one, three, six years after I've worked with them and they pop into my inbox to let me know that they're continuing to make decisions with confidence.

"Sometimes I reference my one-pager / abstract I created during your program and it's all still true. This framework has allowed me to be myself and speak up in service and take personal risk."

"Gaining a Master's is something I have wanted for a long time, but I've held myself back for many reasons. Because of our work together, I am feeling so good about just going for it."

"I decided I needed something new in 2021 and just started another job. Just wanted to let you know that revisiting your framework and the answers that I gave in 2018 was still super helpful and helped me feel secure in making the right decision for my career (and life)!"

"I just wanted to give you a quick update on what I've been doing since we last spoke. I've been in school for a year now and working towards a master's in counseling, and I'll graduate in spring 2020. Starting school and being on the precipice of a new career and new life is amazing and scary, and something I am so grateful for."

"A year later, and while it may not seem like a glamorous job to some, the work is really interesting. I interviewed at some shiny companies for some shiny roles, but I knew in my gut those things weren't what I wanted or needed. I so appreciate you helping people define and find success for themselves."

And clients keep jumping into more and more fulfilling opportunities because they know how to discern if it's going to be a good fit. In one case, they used the skills they've learned to be incredibly clear and confident about purchasing a house and a car—even *I* was surprised by that outcome! And they also give themselves the grace to change their minds at any point in the future, knowing that this is the right decision for them at this moment.

Most importantly, they're alive in their life.

Celebrate where you are today, the courageous decision you've made, and the aliveness you've rekindled in your life.

And then get even more excited for a lifetime of doing what's right for you.

WORK WITH LINDSAY GORDON

1-on-1 Mentorship

The Career Intensive is a 3-month program for senior leaders who have invested many years at their company and are evaluating a possible career change. The program is designed to get you out of feeling stuck, experiencing diminishing returns, and unable to articulate what you want and into feeling clear and confident about what's right for you. By the end of the program, you'll have a decision that's right for you, the experience of a clear conversation with leadership, and an incredibly tailored framework that allows you to make future decisions with unshakeable confidence. Visit www.alifeofoptions.com/career-intensive to learn more.

Join the online course, Job Search Synergy

Job Search Synergy is a self-paced program designed to help you align your work and life goals and reclaim your agency in your next career move. You'll experience a clear and confident job search no matter what stage of the process you're in— assessing offers, just getting started in the search, or wondering if you truly want to quit and launch a full-on job search. Visit www.alifeofoptions.com/work-with-me to learn more.

Book Lindsay for a workshop or company training

Lindsay delivers practical and hands-on workshops that help employees gain clarity about what they want, build confidence in their career decisions, and effectively communicate what they need for job fulfillment to their managers. Lindsay also helps HR leaders retain and re-energize their employees by sharing what truly makes a difference when people choose to re-engage with their existing roles. For more information about these workshops or a custom workshop/training, please email contact@alifeofoptions.com.

Book Lindsay to speak at your event

Lindsay has spoken to audiences at the Grace Hopper Celebration, company summits, conferences and university campuses about how to do what's right for you in your career. To learn more and submit a speaking request, please visit www.alifeofoptions.com/speaking.

FIND LINDSAY GORDON ONLINE

Website: www.alifeofoptions.com
Linkedin: https://www.linkedin.com/in/lindsaygordon/
Email: lindsay@alifeofoptions.com

ABOUT THE AUTHOR

Lindsay is an award-winning career coach for analytically-minded people. She has helped thousands of people do what's right for them in their careers.

She prides herself on helping structure peoples' thinking so that they can make a decision they know they'll be happy with and move forward with confidence. She finds it deeply satisfying and extremely important to deliver her clients "deeply unsexy results" that mean nothing to an outsider but everything to the individual. She knows the frameworks and mindset shifts needed to achieve clarity about what you want, confidence in your decisions, and excitement and energy about the future. Lindsay is proud to have used her practical and structured approach to help leaders do what's right for them and companies to retain and engage their employees.

Lindsay has worked with thousands of people at companies including Apple, Johnson & Johnson, Boeing, CBS, Google, Wells Fargo, Mars, and iRobot. With her guidance and frameworks, more than 50 percent of her clients don't quit the job they're in and 100 percent make a confident decision that is right for them.

Lindsay started her career working as a recycled water engineer in Melbourne, Australia before landing at Google doing technical support for the Google Apps team. After five years of technical support, she transitioned into career development on the Google Cloud team before starting her own business.

In 2021, Lindsay was named to the Forbes Next 1000 list (for upstart entrepreneurs redefining the American dream) and she has been featured in publications and podcasts such as Business Insider, Thrive Global, How to Be Awesome at Your Job, and Side Hustle School. Lindsay holds a BS in Bioengineering from The Franklin W. Olin College of Engineering, a Core Strengths Coaching Certificate from San Francisco State University, and is a Gallup Certified Strengths Coach.

Lindsay loves baking complicated pastries, barbershop singing, and applying her engineering brain to helping people be DECIDED.

To find out more about Lindsay, visit her website www.alifeofoptions.com

ACKNOWLEDGEMENTS

In a world where we can glorify entrepreneurship and individualism, let me be clear that for me, running a business has always been a team effort. I would never have gotten this far without the love, support, and belief of so many people.

To my sweet Brian, this life is an incredibly fun adventure with you. Thank you for supporting me as I figure out this wild ride of running a business and for helping me weather the ups and downs.

To my family, Julie, Scott, Cameron, Tamsin, Wen, Meiling, and Sara. Thanks for always supporting my endeavors, listening to my podcast episodes, and sharing my enthusiasm for what I'm getting up to in the world. To Robin and Kim, thank you for being examples of what it looks like to run a business for decades and for reminding me that the slow times in business never really end, you just get better at riding the waves.

To my bestie Megan, you have enriched my life in countless ways. Thank you for your immense belief in me, your big visions of what's possible in the world, and the energy and excitement you bring to life.

To my chosen colleagues and fellow women business owners, thank you for always being an incredible community of support.

To my coaches along the way, Julie, Emily, and Amira, thank you for helping me find and hone my contribution to the world. Amira, thank you for helping me see that it was time to get my book out into the world.

To Alyssa, thank you for ensuring that this book will resonate with and support as many people as possible. I appreciate all the work we've done together to grow me as a business owner and human.

To Mona, thanks for being an epic part of my team and making everything I do look good.

To Rachel Rodgers, C. René Washington, and Dr. La Tondra Murray, thank you for creating the most incredible community experience and inspiring vision for the future that I have ever seen.

To Jenae, Megan, Julie, Debbie, Becca, Alice, Linda, and Suzanne, thank you for letting me borrow your belief in me as I wrote my first draft.

To Dave, Davina, and the IBW team, thank you for your enthusiasm, support, and care in this process. You are doing life-changing and world-changing work.

And to my first few clients who took a chance on me, thank you for the biggest adventure of my life.